Flood Logic

A Memoir Told in Fragments

Ashley Aldous Pangborn

DISCLAIMER

This book is a memoir reflecting the author's recollections of experiences over time. Some names and identifying details have been changed to protect the privacy of individuals. Some events have been compressed or reordered for narrative purposes. Dialogue represents the author's recollection of the substance of conversations and may not be word-for-word accurate. The author has made every effort to ensure the accuracy of the information presented, but memory is imperfect and subjective.

The strategies and opinions described are the author's personal experience and interpretation of information and are not intended as legal, financial, medical, or structural-engineering advice. Readers should consult qualified professionals for guidance on their situations.

This memoir includes discussions of trauma recovery within a narrative of survival and adaption, including non-graphic reference to past sexual assault.

ISBN 979-8-9999826-0-5
Published by Ashley Aldous Pangborn
Cover Design by Kim Diep

DEDICATION

For Landon and Fay,

When you read this, I hope you feel how fiercely I love you both and how hard I tried to protect your peace. You are the pulse behind every page and the home I never lost.

I love you to the moon and back, around the world, a million times infinity, plus 1.

Mom

***

And to my husband Greg,

For the weight you carried, the trenches we dug, and your quiet steadiness that held when the walls didn't. This book is the chaos we survived and the rhythm we rebuilt in the dark.

Forever and always,

Ashley

CONTENTS

PREFACE

This isn't the kind of story that comes with a clean arc.
There is no tidy beginning, middle, or end.

I wanted that.
I still do.
But that's not what happened.

What happened was, we lived through it...
Twice.

Two hurricanes flooded our home on the Gulf Coast of Florida, north
of Tampa, in just over a year. Hurricane Idalia hit in August 2023.
Thirteen months later, Hurricane Helene arrived. And the devastation
didn't stop just because the rain did.

What happened was, we rebuilt.
And we broke in more ways than one.

Then we rebuilt again.
But this time, from the inside out.

You might wish for more light moments.
So did I.

You might want to see more resolution.
So do I.

This is what it looks like to keep going when everything you counted
on gives out beneath you.

This is what it looks like when survival is quiet.
When the cavalry you wanted doesn't come or can't stay.
When the reporters move on to the next story.
When viewers change the channel.
When you learn to carry the aftermath because no one else will.

And when you start writing in the middle of it all unfolding.

I spend a lot of time inside my head.
Come join me.

Welcome to Flood Logic.
This is what remains.

1

Plan E, Version Two

Prepared but never ready.

"No! Mom, why is this happening to us again?" our daughter, Fay, cries out.

"Honey, it will be okay. We will be okay. But right now, I need you to go to your room and lift all of your things," I tell her.

I make eye contact with our son Landon across the hall. His face is blank, but he nods and moves toward his little sister. "It's okay Fay, we will lift everything, we will save more this time." he says, as they head into their bedrooms, gathering their most cherished belongings.

The news currently predicts there is six to eight feet of storm surge heading to our area. I think I would be even more frantic if this had been the first time we'd read these words.

But honestly?
We are more prepared this time.

I walk into my husband's office and tell him the news. I close my eyes, take a deep breath, and shut off everything in my head telling me it's time to break down and scream.

There isn't time for panic.
No room for sadness or pity over the current situation.

But anger?
Maybe I can use that.
A surge of adrenaline to be used for what lies ahead.

I rush to the kitchen. *I'm not about to rebuy all these small kitchen items.*

Not again.

When you think about the high-value objects in your home, you might assume it's mostly the electronics. But if you do the math, calculate the cost of each item along with its size and storage needs, you quickly realize how fast those little kitchen gadgets, utensils, and accessories add up. I can fill a Rubbermaid tote with hundreds of dollars' worth of essentials in under five minutes.

I clear the countertops and start consolidating, pulling out lower drawers and placing them on higher surfaces. This is the prep work for packing it all up later. I unplug the microwave and coffee maker. *These two things will be essential in my future temporary kitchen.*

I move onto locating our essential documents and most important keepsakes, already packed away in waterproof storage. I take out my insurance documents, social security cards, birth certificates, marriage certificate, house and insurance paperwork and place them in my overnight bag by the front door. I grab my phone and begin photographing as much as I can of the interior and exterior of the home.

Luckily,
or maybe not, but I'm going to go with it,
a good amount of our things are already stored in totes.

We were getting ready to put the house on the market next week. I had just finished staging it after a year-long home renovation we did ourselves, a restoration project following last year's flood from

Hurricane Idalia.

Did I mention we did almost the entire rebuild ourselves?

My hands have touched every piece of material reinstalled in this house.

Deep in my bones, I know,
I just know,
I will be tearing it all out again.

When you go through something traumatic, it's hard not to worry it will happen again. Well-meaning people in your life will try to support you in the ways they know how. But unless they've been through what you have or are some kind of expert in the specific trauma you have experienced, most will never truly understand.

They say things like:

You are so strong.
Like I had a choice.
You've made it through.
As if that means it's over.
It can't possibly happen again.
But it can. And it will.
The worst is behind you.
You don't know that.
Focus on the future.
What if I am? What if that's why I know better?

Here's the thing, I'm not wired like most people. My mind works differently. It's something I've struggled with. It is something which frustrates me more often than I would like to admit. *For most of my life, I've felt like it holds me back.*

Right now, though? My autistic brain is what will get me through this.

I've been crunching the statistics for a year now. Numbers and math usually soothe me, but in this case, they serve as informed preparation. When I told people I knew this would happen again, that it was a matter of when, not if. That the only "if" was whether or not we would still be here when it did...

They called it a trauma response. Fear, hopelessness and despair.

What they couldn't see was,
that it wasn't self-pity.
It wasn't negativity.

It was pragmatism.

If they had been crunching the numbers, if they had been following the statistics, the science, the locality factors... maybe they would have felt differently.

Maybe they wouldn't have kept telling me:
"Just don't think that way."
"Stay positive."

Being stubborn, *as some may call it,* I wouldn't let it go. I had been preparing for this scenario since the last flood. Since the moment we started rebuilding. The web of paths to take, the plans and backup plans, and backups for my backups. They are always being spun in my head, constantly shifting, adapting to new information.

To outsiders, it might look like overthinking.
But to me, it's just thinking.

What's happening now though, this is why I strategize.
This is why I plan, with contingency versions.

PLAN E, Version Two in action:

We have finished rebuilding our home, but it is peak hurricane season again. The building permit closed last week. The final installment of the insurance money from our Idalia flood claim was released to us last month. We still have a mortgage we can't afford to pay off without a sale. The realtor has been chosen but the house hasn't been listed yet. Packing has begun. A storage POD sits on our front lawn.

And the water is coming.
Again.

2.

Against the Water

"I'm not sure how I'm supposed to keep over ten feet of water out of my house." I texted someone, half-joking, half-daring the universe to blink first.

It was hurricane season again.
In Florida, it sometimes feels like it always is.

There's a joke that we have four seasons: summer, more summer, hurricane season, and Christmas lights on palm trees.

But there's no real punchline when you know what it's like to live through a hurricane. *When you know what it's like to have lost everything and still have to get up and prepare to lose it again.*

The thing about hurricane season is, for people like us who live here, it's not an event.

It's a ritual.

We stock our essential hurricane supplies year-round. Buying water, canned food, battery packs, crank radios, flashlights, and fans for when the air turns still and the AC dies. We keep go-bags ready with our paperwork in large Ziploc baggies. Test generators throughout the year. We have evacuation plans, rendezvous points, and communication trees already drawn out like battle strategies.

During peak season the additional prep starts small, because it always does.

Watching the forecasts daily. Tracking the storm model updates when they appear. Waiting for local sightings of the Weather Channel's meteorologist Jim Cantore to surface ...*as most Floridians do.*

Trying to tell the difference between a blip and a threat, when both come wrapped in the same media-issued tone of urgency.

We had doubled down on our prepping for peak hurricane season early this summer. It was the only thing which helped with the nausea that came every time I heard the word "storm." I had bought extra flood barriers in batches, tucked them away like someone stocking a bunker. Slowly, quietly, almost superstitiously.

We were ready.
As ready as anyone could be, given the circumstances.

***

I've always been the one who tracks the forecasts. Who lays out plans. It made sense. Before all of this, I worked in operations and finance. I was used to keeping other people's systems running.

Now I kept my own family moving forward, even as our world unraveled beneath us.

Storm surge predictions had just increased to over twelve feet.

I shifted the plan once again.

My husband had filled 70 sandbags at the county fill station downtown. Sweat pouring off him, working in the heavy, soupy air that makes breathing feel like swallowing syrup. 70 sandbags looked impressive stacked in our driveway, after unloading the trunk of our SUV for the third time. Laid flat around only the exterior doors, they made a three-inch-high wall.

Three inches of hope against over ten feet of water.

It wasn't enough.
It never would be.

We gathered more sandbags from a friend on higher land. We installed the water-filled flood barriers around the doors as well. I painted flood sealant on the thresholds, laid thick flood tape along every seam of the doors. We built sump pump stations at the front and back entrances, that we prayed would buy us time if the river came inside.

We dug a trench around the whole perimeter of the house. Laid thick plastic sheeting against the foundation, stapled it to the wood siding, and pinned it into the earth with corrugated plastic panels.

It looked insane.
It looked desperate.
It was both.

It took six brutal days to finish. Six days in the crushing Florida summer heat. Stopping every hour to sit under the shade and sip lukewarm electrolyte drinks that barely made a dent. No amount of hydrating could replace what the heat took from us.

Last year, I did most of the prep alone. While my husband stayed stuck at his job, unable to leave his desk until the storm was approaching our doorstep.

Now, Greg's hands were beside mine. We were coordinated. Grim, but moving like a team. Maybe not cheerfully, *but together.*

Inside the house, we continued lifting everything we could.

Electronics, furniture, appliances, anything that could be potentially saved if the storm shifted or weakened, elevated off the ground. Chairs stacked on tables, boxes laid on top of the lifted fridge and stove, bins packed and shoved into the loft. We unplugged sockets, turned off breakers, set up raised battery backups, trying to dodge the next power surge.

The house looked like it was mid-evacuation, long before we even finished.

But the house wasn't enough.

Out on the front lawn sat a giant metal storage POD we had rented when we started prepping to sell the house. Back when we thought the worst was behind us.

Now it had become another battlefield.

We had filled it wall to wall with boxes and extra furniture. Everything we had packed away in hopes of staging a clean, perfect home for someone else to someday live in.

We had stacked everything inside the container on folding tables in case this moment ever came. An extra 2 feet high of security. Still, we knew it may not be enough, we couldn't unload everything in time. *Where would we even put any of it? It wasn't going to be much safer indoors.*

So we strapped it all tight against the storage container's walls with bungee cords and ropes until it looked like a spiderweb of desperation.

Every table, every chair, every bin was latched down, double-checked, then triple-checked. Not because it made the Pod invincible, but because we needed to believe we could still do something.

But it didn't look strong enough.

Nothing did.
Paranoia sang under every knot we tied.
Every rope we pulled tighter.

What if it's not enough?
What if it floats away?
What if everything we've saved breaks free and drowns without us?

There are few things more hollow than trying to save what you already know is lost.

Our neighbor Steve came over after finishing his own house prep. He helped us build the final flood barriers.

Our friend Sarah came too. Lifting boxes, carrying books, picking out clothes and cooking pans to save. She packed her car with as much of our life as she could fit to ferry inland.

Sarah's house was just a twenty minute drive away from the river beside our home. Not far. But last year we learned, twenty minutes could mean a whole different reality.

She invited us to stay with her family again ...*well, more like insisted on it before we could even ask.* Sarah, her husband Roger, and their son Cooper had already prepared a space for us.

They weren't in a flood zone.
Their roads didn't swell into rivers.
Their home didn't move like it was breathing under pressure.

This is where we were evacuating to. It was far enough to be considered safe and close enough that we could still return to the house as quickly as needed once the hurricane passed.

***

21

Every hurricane season we field the frantic calls and texts.
"Please leave!"
"Are you going to evacuate?"
"Where will you go? Please get as far away as possible!"

"Think about the kids."

As if we weren't already thinking about them.
As if we ever stopped.

The concerned outsiders don't see us tracking, making calculations, and whispering late-night contingency plans over maps. After over a decade living in Florida, we know things outsiders don't.

Evacuating isn't a button you just push.

It's an informed gamble. Leave too early, and the storm could turn and chase you into a worse disaster. Go north, it could curve. Go south, it could ricochet back. Go across the state too soon, it could follow you there too. Go too late and risk getting trapped in gridlock, stuck in your car with your kids when the wind hits.

And then there's gas shortages and people having to leave cars stranded on the side of highways. There's a small window where decisions actually make sense *and it's narrow.* Fractured by forecast shifts and road closures and infrastructure that collapses under the weight of a million fleeing souls.

Then there's the expense of evacuating "far enough away."
We save all year for the possibility.

We're lucky we can.

Not every family can afford to leave. Not every family even gets the time off work to try. But even compromising and evacuating locally to designated public shelters isn't magic. I've seen the roofs of shelters peeled back like tuna cans.

I've learned to tell people early now. "We know." "We're watching." "We're preparing. I'll update you." "Trust us."

Trust, we want to live just as badly as they want us to.
Trust, we are thinking about our children every second.
Trust, that no one will protect us better than we will.

This is our home.
Our family.
Our lives.

No one else will pick up all the pieces afterwards. No one else will stand in the wreckage explaining to our kids how we lost everything. Again.

And this time, the stakes feel sharper.

Not just because of the flood maps or the forecasts or the endless doom loops on TV, but because we know what it really costs now. The price of survival isn't just measured in luck. It's measured in the breathless silence afterward and the hollowed-out spaces you have to live in.

Even if you make it.
Especially if you make it.

3.

Built by Storms

We arrived by mid-afternoon. Sarah opened the door like we belonged there.

We headed to the guest bedroom. The kids set up their spot on an air mattress. Our cat found a pile of laundry and made it his. Greg and I collapsed on the bed from exhaustion. All of us, together in one room. A borrowed space. A stitched-together version of safety.

Outside, the sky dimmed and the storm moved in. But we weren't afraid of the wind. We had learned by now, the wind is just the beginning. The damage doesn't come in gusts for us.

It comes during the quiet exhale.

I thought about our house. Just last week, it had finally felt like it was healed from Hurricane Idalia. The walls were rebuilt. Floors repaired. Fresh paint. New lights. Even the smallest staging details like the framed chalkboard sign reading, "Welcome to your new home!" placed just so.

It felt like we were already halfway out the door. Hands on the doorknob ready to open it for new owners.

We had scrubbed it of our grief.
We had made it clean enough to leave.

And now, here we were, lying in a friend's guest bed.
Hoping we could still escape in the morning.

I watched the fan spin shadows on the ceiling. Greg beside me. Quiet.
Still. But I could feel the tension in him, a current under the stillness.
He was trying to sleep. *I was trying to pretend I could.*

I kept thinking about the last time. How, for a full year, I stayed moving.
My hands busy, eyes forward. How he folded inward under the weight
of it all.

We were built different.
Not better. Not worse.
Just... different.

His trauma taught him to retreat.
Mine taught me to scan. To fix.

The last time this happened, we pulled apart, in ways I never thought
possible. Since then, we have worked our way back. Not all the way but
enough. Enough to be holding hands in the dark again. I worried what
another hit would mean.

Not just to the house,
but to us.

To the thread we'd been slowly reweaving. To the tenderness which had
only just begun to return. Would we bend again? Or would we finally
break?

He reached for my hand.
I squeezed back.
Not a promise.
A presence.

And in that moment, it had to be enough.

The storm passed overhead.
Branches hit the roof.
Phones buzzed.
Power flickered.

But we had been through worse. When the radar cleared, we exhaled, but only halfway. Because we didn't need forecasts to tell us what came next. *The body remembers what radar can't.*

Last time, we thought we were safe once the wind was gone. But the damaging water didn't come with the storm's wind and rain. The surge came after. It rose while we were sleeping. After we had celebrated our home surviving the landfall. It came when no one was watching. When we thought the worst was over.

So I watched.

I stayed awake while my family drifted.
Kept my phone beside me, glowing faint blue against the dark.

At first, the updates were manageable. Minor street flooding. Puddles in places we expected them. We might be okay. *If it didn't get worse.* But I knew, I knew the water kept coming, long after the clouds moved on. I knew, not to embrace a sense of relief too early.

I lay in the dark, waiting to hear what we already feared.

Early morning came before the sun. Everyone else, still sleeping. The room was warm with shared breath and collective body heat. Our cat stretched against our legs. I sat upright, watching the messages roll in. Water inching up driveways submerging mailboxes. A picture of our road, already half engulfed by the river water that had swelled and crept inland.

My neighbor messaged me. He was waiting for sunrise. He would send a photo when he could see clearly. When it came, I stared at it for a long time.

Our house.
Submerged deeper than last year.

The message under the photo said:
"We woke up to an eel in our living room."

Something in me locked up. Not numb really, just pressurized. I set my
phone face down beside me and lay back into the subtle noise of my
family breathing.

Everything that mattered was in this room.
Everything else...
was gone again.

I had been built by storms.
But it didn't mean I didn't feel the breaking.

4

Deja Vu but Different

We left the kids at Sarah and Roger's. They were playing a board game, still in pajamas, still laughing. They didn't need to see this yet. At least we could protect them from owning this memory.

We didn't even get close with our initial attempt to get home.

There was no dramatic entrance.

Just a slow crawl from neighborhood to neighborhood, detour after detour, until we realized the roads had disappeared again. Not just our street, the routes to our street. Block after block still submerged. Intersections vanished. GPS turned useless.

We weren't going to make it.

Instead we tried to act like it was a reconnaissance run, like we were only scoping the damage. But both of us knew the truth. We were trying to go home. We were trying to face it. We were trying to beat the mold, the heat, the hours turning floodwater into rot. We needed to start mitigating the damage before it spread beyond the range our insurance would cover.

But we couldn't even get close enough to fail properly.

Last year, at least, we had a kayak. A plan. A way in. I remember clutching the front of the borrowed kayak hanging out of the SUV's open trunk. Greg driving slowly while I gripped the edge like it might float us out of denial.

We announced ourselves to invisible neighbors just in case someone thought looters moved in with paddle gear.

"Don't shoot."
"It's Ashley and Greg."

We had slipped through our community park like ghosts, paddling over what used to be a walking path. We stepped across long floating logs like tightropes to reach our yard. And waded through the rest until we reached our side door.

It was terrifying.
It was ridiculous.
It worked.

This time?

There was no point bringing a kayak. We couldn't even get within walking distance of where we needed to start. We had to turn around. We didn't say much.

I remember Greg tapping the steering wheel, not out of rhythm, but out of control. I sat still. Too still. A tight, heavy silence between us where mourning lives when it hasn't been identified yet.

Our second attempt was different.

The water had pulled back, like it knew we were coming. Not all the way. Not safely. Just enough to make the decision harder.

We knew what we were driving into. We knew the SUV might not forgive us. The roads weren't dry, just less underwater. The floodwaters still lingered and the mud and water could still trap us. But we also knew, every hour counted. Once the water left, it didn't mean the damage stopped.

It meant it started.

Mold blooms. Wood swells. Floors crack. Smells seep into walls like sensory stains. Saltwater rusts the tools you will need to pull it all out before it spreads too far. Every minute we waited was another minute of loss settling deeper into the bones of the house. So we kept driving. We kept pushing through.

I don't remember exactly when we crossed the line from "maybe..." to "definitely." Only that my heart clenched when I saw the street sign bent at an angle, familiar and wrong. The houses were silent. *Like they knew.* No movement. No people. Just debris clinging to fences and trees like aftermath confetti.

We turned down our road. I remember counting how many houses we passed before I had to stop breathing through my nose. It wasn't far. And then, there it was.

Our house.
Still standing.
But something not right.

You learn how to tell.

The angles are wrong. The color of the siding changes just slightly when it's soaked through. The shape of the windows shifts under pressure. *You know.*

The front door was warped. The whole yard was coated in a layer of silt, like someone had dragged a river through our yard. *Well, I guess that's exactly what mother nature had done.* Our flood barriers were carried to places we didn't put them. The large storage POD shifted to a new location on our lawn.

There were no footprints. No signs of entry. Just the strange post-flood stillness. The quiet which comes after disaster.

Where the world is stuck in a pause, pretending it didn't break you.

We stepped out of the SUV.
No kayak.
No gear.
Just our feet sinking into thick, slippery mud.

5.

Mopping a Declaration

The second time, we didn't panic.
We didn't rush.
Not because we weren't devastated because we were.

This wasn't the same kind of shock as before.
This was recognition.

I cautiously stepped over the stacks of sandbags and stood by the swollen door, fingers hovering above the handle.

You could see the scum line, a dark, gritty outline that wraps around the house like a noose.

It told us everything.

How high the water climbed.
How long it sat.
How deep the damage went.

We hadn't even opened the door yet, and I was already unraveling the mystery.

Greg said something, maybe a curse, maybe my name, but I didn't hear it. I just stared at the line. Like it might answer the question I hadn't spoken yet.

Why again?

The lock turned and the frame resisted. The door began to open. *But not really.*

I peered through the hazy glass and saw it. A wall of our own belongings. Storage containers and boxes, shoved and tangled, pressed violently against the door. Thrown there by the water itself.

The house didn't want to let us in.

I stuck my arm through the crack, nudging anything I could reach. Then my leg, bracing against the swollen frame, kicking just enough space to squeeze through. My skin slid against muck and sand. My pants caught on a popped nail, sharp and unapologetic, jutting from the frame like a warning.

"I'm in!" I called, voice shaking more than I expected.

I cleared a path just wide enough for Greg to follow, moving like someone trained in crisis.

Because I was.
Because we both were.

We pulled out our phones.
Started filming.

It felt wrong. To be recording it. Like we were memorializing the moment instead of living it. Like we were walking through the death scene of something we had built with our own hands.

But we knew better now.

I had already opened a claim with our insurance before we even returned to the house. It was anyone's guess when we would be

34

assigned an adjuster or when an inspection would be scheduled. It could be days, even weeks. Given the amount of widespread damage throughout Florida and up the coast, we knew the number of claims would be stacking.

They were going to fight us on what they would cover.
We needed proof.

Proof of what we saw, exactly as we found it. Before anything was moved, or touched, or swept away. Before the story could be questioned.

We were securing the scene like detectives. Careful not to break the chain of custody on our own life. This wasn't just documentation.

It was a defense.
A case file.
An archive.
A quiet war.

Because the burden would be on us. *Again.*

To prove what we lost.
To prove we didn't cause it.
To prove we were telling the truth.

Even before the system came for us, we were already bracing. Already building our case. Already defending ourselves in the only way we could. Because we knew what they needed, what they'd look for, and what they'd try to twist. You don't wait to be accused when you've already lived through being dismissed.

You gather your evidence.
You prepare to advocate.
You act like you're representing yourself in open court...
because you might as well be.

The first flood from last year had shocked us. There's no preparing for the first time you see water crawl into your house like it owns the place. No way to process what it means to watch the walls blister and the couch buckle under the weight of the water still stuck inside it. The air full with a smell you'll never forget.

No one tells you how quiet a house becomes when it's trying not to fall apart in front of you.

After Idalia, the distress came loud.
Sudden.
Ripping through the body like a rip current.

But this wasn't that.
We were different now.

Inside, it smelled like decay. Like something sacred had died here. Not rot exactly, not yet. The smell of rot takes a little longer to settle in. This was the pungent tang of low tide and heat-stewed debris. Silt and drywall. Wet insulation, septic backup, and flooded earth. You could almost taste it just from inhaling.

The real anguish this time wasn't in what we'd lost.
It was in what we'd almost saved.

We were so close.
The house was finished.
Staged.
Listed, almost.

I had patched the missing walls, installed new flooring, replaced the electrical and plumbing, built the new cabinets, installed the vanities, tiled new showers, painted the baseboards, scrubbed and caulked and sanded until it looked like a future again.

We weren't just repairing, we were preparing to leave.

Now it was all back on the ground. Our belongings soaked and our plans stalled. The exit we had fought for had been ripped away.

Just gone.

The floor looked dry *but it wasn't*. The tile was slick with a layered sheen of filth. My rubber sandals squeaked with every step. Not in the way it would sound softly creaking as the plastic shifted on clean tile, but the shrill drag of tension against lost resistance. The noise between suction and slipping of your soles.

I walked carefully, one foot sliding slightly forward.
Testing the ground like it might shift beneath me. Off-camera, I slipped twice. Caught myself both times, barely.

The fridge was toppled behind the kitchen island like a child playing hide and seek. Just barely peeking out. Not violently flung, just slumped like it had tipped over in quiet surrender. It didn't look like a storm had done it.

It looked like it had decided not to get back up.

I stood staring at it.
wondering how long it had held out before falling.

We continued to walk the rooms.
We touched the walls like we were checking a pulse.

The fan in the living room was still on. Ceiling blades turning gently overhead, spinning above a room full of ruined things. It made no sense. The power had held but the walls hadn't.

The contradiction of it, almost made me laugh.

The house was saying enough without words as each room greeted us like a repeat of a bad dream. Except the dream had changed, just enough to make it worse. Just enough to be jealous of last year's damage.

We moved through the house with purpose.
We knew the order already:

Turn off the compromised electrical breakers.
Immediately remove the HVAC filters so the AC doesn't stall out.
Identify what was saved and safe.
Find what was salvageable.
Pull out the sump pumps and shop vacs, the squeegees, mops, towels, and contractor trash bags.

We started carrying out the soaked and ruined personal belongings. Placed the fans and dehumidifiers immediately, when a spot was cleared. Plugged them into untouched outlets on safe independent electrical wire runs and battery backups.

I grabbed the mop and started cleaning.

But not before defiantly mopping the phrase "F THIS!" in what used to be our living room.

The white tile showing through the thick dark muck made the letters visible. I chuckled to myself and snapped a picture. I called Greg over to show off my masterpiece. He raised an eyebrow like he wasn't sure whether to be impressed or worried. I shrugged.

It was either this or scream into a shop vac.

The tears stayed somewhere behind my eyeballs, unmoving, like floodwater held back by sandbags. This wasn't the kind of devastation that empties you. This was the kind that fills you up too fast and stays there. Your body becomes heavy and waterlogged. It wasn't just the house that had flooded again.

It was us.

The second time doesn't soften the blow.
It just changes how it lands.

Now, we moved with the knowledge of what came next.
...With a few small surprises along the way.

I hadn't found them yet. The minnows. *But I would.*

Six of them, eventually. Small silver bodies embedded in the muck. Little signs that the river had been inside. That it had swum through the walls and over the tile and across the place where we used to eat breakfast. I would find them while squeegee-ing the mud into scoopable piles. I would shovel their corpses into buckets and carry them back outside.

Where the mud belonged.

Their eyes still glassy.
Still staring.

6.

The Floor is Lava

Have you ever played the game The Floor is Lava?
I used to hop from pillow to pillow,
from couch to chair with my sister.

Imagine now,
everything that touches the floor
has become lava too.

What would be left?
To balance on,
to cling to?

What if, instead,
everything that touched the ground
was destroyed by water?

That's when you realize
how connected everything is to the floor.

Your furniture rests on it.
Your appliances too.

Everything that gave order to chaos.
Bookshelves, cabinets, and desks.
Everything that held us while we slept.
Bed frames and their matching nightstands.

Doors.
Fireplaces.
Rugs.

Even the curtains
were purposely hung,
to graze the floor gently.

A few inches of saltwater,
ruins more than you'd think.
A few feet of it
Finishes what the inches started.

The baseboards.
The walls that touch them.
The things with nowhere to hang,
tucked in closets and forgotten corners.

Toys and shoes,
left scattered after use.

The ground might as well have been lava.
It swallowed it all.

And if the ground had surrendered,
what would stop us from falling?

7.

Buttered Noodles

*The kids were still dripping from the pool when we walked back into
Sarah and Roger's.*

Their makeshift fort stretched across the back porch, towels draped
over chairs, couch cushions stacked like battlements. Fay, Cooper, and
Landon huddled inside, laughing, water still clinging to their skin. The
smell of chlorine still in their hair.

We didn't interrupt them. Roger looked up from the kitchen, Sarah,
from the hallway. We answered their unspoken question with a head
shake and a long exhale.

"It's bad."
We murmured quietly enough not to break the moment.

No collapse.
No panic.

Just a kind of quiet choreography of two people who'd seen storms up
close before and knew better than to let distress land too loud in a place
where children were still playing.

We peeled off our contaminated outer layers of clothing and left our
shoes by the door. Mud-caked soles. Salt-brined hems. One by one,
we took turns scrubbing the day off our skin. Soap, hot water, fresh
clothes. Rituals of control in a life no longer offering any.

When we were clean again, we crouched in front of the kids.

No big speech.
Just presence.

They already knew. Not the specifics, but the shape of it. They nodded, blinked, shook it off the way kids sometimes can. *There wasn't anything they could do and sadness wouldn't bring their house back to what it was.*

Sarah came in and asked if we were up for something comforting. "Buttered noodles?" A staple in both our households. A soft, starchy form of mercy.

"Yes!" the kids said in unison. The men nodded.
I didn't try to hide my relief.

Something safe.
Something easy.
Something which wouldn't fall apart under pressure.

After a flood, your brain goes primal. You stop thinking ahead and focus only on what's right in front of you.

Maybe that wasn't fully true for me because on some level, planning had become a survival reflex too.

Reverting to your reptilian brain may be a trauma response but it's also practical.

You need water. You need food. You need dry clothes and a clean towel. *You need to feel human.* You can't afford to think about what's next. When the structure of your day collapses, you build a new one around the few things you can control. Some days that's food. Or coffee. Or changing into a clean shirt, even if it's the only clean shirt you have left.

You learn your family's comfort foods. What tastes bring them back into their bodies. For us, it's buttered noodles. They don't even need sauce. There's something about the salt, the starch, the buttery texture that holds the memory of home. After the first flood, it's what got our daughter to eat again. Buttered noodles meant maybe everything wasn't broken.

After dinner, while the kids built a second fort and the dishes soaked, Greg and I ducked into the guest room to book our first rental. We needed to act quickly before the listings vanished. We found one with enough room for us, the cat, and space for my aunt. She'd already been preparing to come before the storm even hit. She knew before we did, that we'd need her.

When we stepped back into the hallway, Sarah was doing our laundry. Quietly folding shirts into neat stacks. "If you keep this up..." I said. "We might never leave." She laughed, didn't look up. Just kept folding.

We didn't know Sarah and Roger for very long before the hurricanes hit. Maybe a few playdates. Some texts. The cautious early-stage friendship where you're still learning each other's rhythms. More than acquaintances, not yet best friends. Somewhere in the hopeful middle ground.

Honestly, I barely knew Roger at all. But when Idalia hit, when we evacuated to a hotel, watched the storm track shift, and got the call that our house had flooded, they opened their home to us.

No questions.
No hesitation.

When checkout time loomed and we didn't know where else to go, they made the decision for us: "Come here."

They didn't just offer shelter. They offered us dignity when it didn't feel like we had much left. They didn't pity us. They didn't act like they were doing us a favor. They saw us hollowed out, cracked open and simply said,

"Stay."

They fed us. Made space for our heartbreak without trying to shrink it. They let the kids be loud and let us be quiet. And when the immediate sorrow faded, they gave us something harder to name, a place to feel normal again.

It would have been enough.
But it didn't stop there.

Our friendship kept growing.
Not quickly. Not loudly.
But steadily.
With weight.

And when Helene came the next year, after the trenches and sandbags and the tape and heat, Sarah showed up again. Not because she had to. Because it's who she is.

There's a kind of friendship which grows in disaster. Not because of the trauma but because of what survives it.

The kind that doesn't need performance.
That doesn't mistake stillness for distance.
That knows presence matters more than solutions.

Maybe part of why it worked, *still works*, is because we're built from some of the same pieces. There's no need for subtext. No cautious translation. No wondering if silence means something it doesn't. It's one of the easiest friendships I've ever had. And somehow one of the strongest. It made me question what I'd convinced myself I deserved.

What I had learned to accept. Connections which often burned too fast or vanished as soon as things got hard or I became less useful.

With Sarah, I don't have to shrink. I don't have to explain. We support each other without keeping score. We sit in the mess together, without needing to fix it. We let the silence be what it is. Sometimes presence is more than enough.

Sometimes it's everything.

I'm not embarrassed to say she has seen the worst parts of me.

The jagged, sharp-edged, unwashed pieces. And I never worry she'll turn them into weapons someday.

We grow beside each other.
Not in competition.
Not out of obligation.
Just... steadily.

It's friendship that doesn't need ceremony. It doesn't require announcements. It just shows up and keeps showing up, like buttered noodles. Simple. Reliable. Comforting in ways you don't even know you needed until it's already on your plate.

It's easy to love someone at their best. It's harder to sit with them in the wreckage. Harder still, to stay when the storm quiets *and everything is just, heavy.*

Sarah stayed.
Roger stayed.

They didn't just help us survive the floods. They had reminded us survival could still be gentle. Survival could still carry love. Still hold joy. Still be worth choosing.

There's a before and after to a friendship like that.

Before you know it's real. And after, when you know you'll never forget it. When I think about what survived the floods, what actually made it through, their friendship is on the list.

8.

Trauma Tower

There's a part of me that's tired even before I start counting.

The hard things.
The small betrayals.

The moments I didn't think I would survive. But did anyway. Compiled one after another, until it stopped feeling worth the energy to keep track.

It's easier not to count them. Easier to let the weight blur together, until it just becomes the air I breathe.

My mind doesn't always do what I want it to. It spirals when I need it to climb. It lingers when I need it to move forward. It presses old wounds open when I'm trying to stitch new ones closed.

And my body, my body has failed me, too.

At the worst moments.
When I needed it most to protect me, to defend me, it didn't.

And even though I know, rationally, being violated all those years ago while on the cusp of adulthood, wasn't my fault, there's still some small, merciless part of me that keeps whispering otherwise. It keeps asking why I couldn't stop it. Even over a decade and a half later, I still ask,

"Why couldn't I save myself?"

Too often, survival carries guilt alongside it. As if staying alive wasn't enough. As if surviving without protecting yourself makes you complicit in your own hurt.

It's not about playing the victim. I've never wanted that. *I've never lived there.* If anything, I've spent my entire life sprinting in the other direction. Building, fixing, and holding others together when I couldn't hold myself. Focusing on what's left after the storms pass, after the worst happens and the dust settles. Focusing on what remains inside of me after the breaking is done.

Or maybe it's never done.
Maybe I just learned how to keep moving anyway.

But here's the part I don't say out loud often:

That feeling.
The one they call "resilience."
The one people point to and say, "You're so strong!"

It's fragile.
It's fleeting.

It doesn't stick the way they think it does.

It's a fracture which hasn't been mended properly.
Strong enough to bear weight, but tender every time you shift too suddenly.

Every time I think I've made it through, every time I dare to feel steady again, something new comes along and knocks the breath out of my chest. Life has a way of whispering when I'm not ready, "You thought you were safe? Think again."

And I do.
Over and over.

I think again. I brace again. I rebuild again.

But each time, the weight gets heavier. Each time, a little more of me gets left behind.

It all gets stacked, layer on top of layer. Each trauma, a block, placed carefully above the last.

Years of them.
Decades.

A tower of survival built piece by piece.

In therapy, I try to unpack them. Nudging what shifts. Testing what loosens. Each session, carefully sliding out one memory, one wound, one negative core belief. Examining it in the light before trying to place it back on top.

But when your life is built on Jenga Blocks, how much reorganization can you sustain before it all comes crashing down?

Sometimes I feel the whole structure sway, when we touch something load-bearing.

My therapist says this is normal. The wobble before finding a new balance. But she doesn't live inside the tower. She doesn't feel how my hands shake. Placing each processed piece back, knowing one wrong move could topple everything I've built to keep myself upright.

But even when the tower holds, even when nothing falls, the fear of collapse never truly leaves.

Because my brain still doesn't heal neatly.

It still circles back when I least expect it.
It gets trapped in places I thought I'd already evacuated.

There are still days I ask myself, not so kindly,

"Why can't you just move on?"
"Why can't you be normal about this?"

But trauma doesn't ask for permission before it rewires you. It just does. And you live inside the new architecture, even when it doesn't fit. Even when it aches.

The more I fight it, the more stuck I get. I know that now, but knowing doesn't unstick me.

There's a version of myself I keep chasing. A version who processes things the right way. Who feels pain, files it neatly, and moves forward without dragging it behind her like overstuffed luggage.

I want to be her.
I want to believe I can become her.

But sometimes, clinging onto that hope feels like another kind of weight. Another unmet expectation I strap to my own back.

The thing about surviving over and over again, is people start to expect it from you. You survived last time. You'll survive this too, right? Like it's a skill you can polish.

But even the strongest muscles fatigue.
Even the most stubborn spirits crack.

There's a burden in resilience.
There's a loneliness in it, too.

When you survive alone, you learn how to carry the weight yourself.

You learn how to patch the roof and hold the walls up while the storm howls outside. You also learn not to expect anyone to stand beside you. You learn sometimes no one's coming with reinforcements.

You are the reinforcements.
You are the roof, the walls, the last defense.

I can't ignore the truth. When I look back at everything I've survived, there are parts of me which never really healed. There are parts that stitched themselves back together wrong. Scar tissue thin where trust should be thick.

Fear, wired too close to hope.

I'm not dismissing the progress I've made. I know what I've survived should have destroyed me. I know I shouldn't even still be here some days. But it's hard not to live half-braced for the next wave. Hard not to wonder when the other shoe will drop. Hard not to scan the horizon for the next shadow heading my way.

Survival taught me how to expect the worst.
Healing is trying to teach me how to expect something more benign.

But it's a slow, uneven lesson.
And some days, the old instincts still win.

9.

Miles of Debris

After Helene, there were donation centers everywhere. Distribution lines formed and volunteer crews came from other towns. Strangers helped cut downed trees and cleared roads. People dropped off bottled water, paper towels, and supplies. We said thank you and meant it. Almost like it didn't feel strange to be helped by the community this time.

This was the community we had been waiting for last year.

After Idalia, most people assumed only the rich flooded. That you had to have a personal dock and a boat and a million-dollar house to be affected. They didn't see themselves in us.

It didn't matter that we had bought the roughest house in the neighborhood and poured ourselves into it, to make it shine. It didn't matter that our street was full of potholes we filled with rocks ourselves or that half our neighbors were retired and on a fixed income. We weren't waterfront luxury. We were just... wet. And not one local who didn't already know us seemed to care.

I remember one day Greg came home from the store deeply discouraged. He had been in line with a cart full of bleach, gloves, extra fans, cleaning rags and other supplies. A woman behind him kept sighing and glancing at her watch then back at his cart. Greg had turned around, sheepish.

"Sorry for the wait," he offered.
"Our house flooded."

She shrugged. "Oh, well mine didn't. I was fine."
That was the end of her empathy... *If you could call it empathy.*

***

Less than a week after Idalia, we walked to the park at the end of our street. Boats were already back on the water. People were swimming. Greg called out a warning. He told them septic tanks in the surrounding neighborhoods had flooded and the water might be unsafe.

They didn't take it well.

A man in the water started screaming at us. Called us names. Told me to go cry somewhere else. Told me no one cared about our kids, when I tried to explain. He told us, if we wanted help, we should shut up and file an insurance claim like everyone else.

By the end of it, I was squatting in the mud at the edge of the community park, sobbing. I had tried to de-escalate the tension. Then I tried to make them see us.

They refused.

This year, the damage reached further. Inland homes flooded too. People who had never been touched by surge or tide were gutting their drywall, piling mattresses on the curb, watching FEMA trucks turn onto their own streets. The suffering had spread more widely, and suddenly, we weren't a cautionary tale. We were fellow survivors.

We were included.

Citizen-led groups began to form across the county. People organized on social media to match volunteers with flooded homes. They brought tools and meals. Helped tear out baseboards. Offered rides and manpower and whatever they could scrounge from their garages. There was effort. There was a sense of community building. The kind of community we hoped for the year before.

***

I drove through town in a daze. It felt like I was seeing it for the first time, though I'd lived here for a few years now.

Last year, there had been homes torn apart, trees uprooted, streets and houses flooded. I thought I'd prepared myself for the piles of debris sitting outside every home. I'd seen it before. But this year, it was different. It wasn't just the destruction on my front lawn or close by anymore. It seemed to be everywhere we went.

Shattered windows, broken drywall, and beds that had once been soft places for children to fall asleep. They all laid matted with mud and soaked in storm surge water.

It was as if the entire town had been laid bare. Each house exposed to the world, their secrets laid out on the street for anyone to see.

There were baby clothes, wedding albums, old holiday decorations curled and melted into piles. Memories soaked through until they collapsed under their own weight.

It felt like being undressed in public.

Every failure, every hope, every fragile thing you'd tried to protect stacked in messy, rotting heaps.

I couldn't help but wonder how we'd gotten here. How all this could have been reduced to so much trash. This mess of belongings, memories, and brokenness. There was something about seeing the debris that hit harder than the storm itself.

But then, sometimes, you'd drive by pockets of normalcy, these little islands of untouched homes, surrounded by the chaos. It felt surreal,

57

like the storm hadn't even grazed them. They had yards with downed tree branches and some debris, but no ruined appliances or soggy cabinets. No shredded beds. No broken toys belonging to children who would never sleep in those beds again.

It was like the world had divided into two.

Devastation on one side.
And normalcy, however fleeting, on the other.

And yet, even in those moments of calm, I couldn't shake the heavy feeling. The storm had already torn through so many lives. Even if their houses were still standing, no one was truly untouched by the damage it caused.

I just couldn't escape the reality of it. There was no getting away from the truth that this storm had stolen so much from us all. *We were in it together this time.*

But I still didn't trust it. Not completely.

There was effort. There was kindness. But there was also a flinch. A part of me kept waiting for it to turn. To be told again we should stop whining. That no one cares. I felt terrible about it. The fact that it took this much pain for us to stop being invisible. So many others had to suffer for us to stop suffering alone.

10.

Bystander's Gaze

There's a moment in every tragedy when people pause, not to help, but to watch.

We call it disaster voyeurism.

You see it in the way we gather around chaos. In how we slow down for car crashes. In the way we pull out our phones to film another person's worst moment. It's not new. It's human nature. We don't want to be responsible, we just want to watch.

It's the bystander's gaze. People driving through neighborhoods they don't live in just to look at the devastation. They film our dismantlement. Our waterlogged furniture. Our heartache, as we hold each other on front lawns, trying to make sense of how our lives just got turned upside down. We can hear them as they crawl by in their vehicles. Pointing their fingers at us, with mouths wide open, saying things like, "Oh wow." "Look at that." "Can you believe it?" "How sad."

They become tourists of tragedy.

People escaping through our devastation like it's part of the entertainment on their hurricane staycation.

They weave slowly through our streets with phones angled out their windows. Narrating our suffering like its content. They upload videos set to music captioned with hashtags.

They tell themselves they're spreading awareness,
and then they leave.

But they don't just leave.
They leave a wake.
Literally.

Their tires push water back toward the homes we're still trying to dry out. They disrupt what little control we've clawed back. Locals hang handmade signs pleading "Please do not create a wake."

We shouldn't have to beg not to be turned into a spectacle. But we do.

Because some people think suffering is interesting.

There's a cost to this kind of tourism. Both a physical one and an emotional one. They get to pass through devastation.

We live in what they leave behind.

11.

Kitchen Triage

And as we work through the water and mud that doesn't get a chance to dry when it's splashed back at us, we are careful. We were extra careful piling the debris.

Not just gloves and goggles and masks, though we wore those too. We moved slowly, deliberately, bent our knees and checked our footing. Warning each other before lifting anything sharp.

We had learned our lesson after Idalia.

Because last time, while loading up a dumpster, Greg stepped back and caught a piece of shattered mirror in his calf.

Deep and unexpected.

He staggered into the house, white as a ghost, drenched in sweat. "I think something bit me!" he said.

We had just seen a cottonmouth snake in the yard near the debris pile, so the possibility didn't feel far-fetched. He laid down on the floor, legs shaking. I ran to grab the first aid kit under the bathroom sink and remembered it had flooded.

Everything I had safely and neatly stored away was gone. Soaked, spoiled, and scattered. All I could find were some crinkled Band-Aids at the bottom of my purse.

Those weren't going to work.

I poured bottled water over his leg. I picked the glass out with tweezers. Doused it with water again. Applied pressure with a clean rag and some paper towels.

I ran to a neighbor's house to see if they had salvaged any emergency medical supplies. They had some peroxide and gauze, which was enough. I ran back, heart beating a mile a minute and cleaned the wound again. Then adhered the gauze with blue painters tape wrapped around his leg.

Greg was silent by then, still sweating. The adrenaline left his body abruptly when he realized it wasn't a snake bite. Just glass. He said he didn't need urgent care. Said he'd be fine despite my protests.

I drove to the store to stock up on more supplies. I rushed into the Publix, right over to the pharmacy. They knew us there. I asked, "Hey, hypothetical question... say my husband got stabbed by a dirty piece of mirror from our flood debris pile... what would I need to treat it, if he refused to go to urgent care?"

The pharmacist shook her head. "Seriously Ashley! You all can't catch a break!" She then walked me through a list of supplies. And pleaded with me to try to get him to change his mind about seeing a doctor because he was going to need antibiotics.

I went back home and re-cleaned and re-bandaged the wound.

Not even two hours later, Steve came over to help with throwing out the debris. I decided to gather all the mirror shards into an old coffee grinds container. I didn't want anyone else to get hurt. *I was trying to be responsible and careful.*

Then I reached over the lip of the container to toss in one last shard, I yelled a 4 letter word while grabbing my arm. I had sliced my forearm open on a sliver sticking just a little too high. It wasn't a graze. It was a clean, unforgiving split. Greg and Steve turned. Greg limped over to check on me, still bleeding himself.

"I'm fine!" I said.
I wasn't.

We went inside. Greg called over Landon.

He had just come back from a summer camp which covered robotics, science labs, and luckily, emergency field triage. They'd taught him how to splint limbs, stop bleeding, and stabilize wounds until help arrived. Apparently, that also applied to moms bleeding on the kitchen floor.

He was calm. Precise. Focused.

I watched as they both worked together. I was so proud I didn't even flinch when they cleaned the cut.

Greg insisted we go to urgent care. He hadn't gone when he was the one hurt, of course not, but this was different. This was now both of us cut by sewage covered debris.

I guess I inadvertently found a way to get him to go. It just took more convincing than I had bargained for.

We left the kids with Lori and Steve then drove to the clinic. I held my arm in the air the whole way, soaked gauze clinging to my arm. They brought me in immediately. *I've never been called back to an examination room so fast here. That made me nervous.*

Liquid stitches. Antibiotics. Compliments on the bandaging. Greg finally got his leg looked at too.

When it was time to pay, the receptionist asked how we'd like to handle the charges. Greg nodded toward me with a smirk on his face and asked if they had a two-for-one special. She didn't laugh. With a straight face she said "No, we don't offer that."

He tilted his head and said "It was a joke!" *I thought it was pretty funny.* I couldn't hold in my amusement as I tried to stop myself from laughing.

Later that night, I went online and bought two snake bite suction kits.

One for the house, stored on the highest shelf we had, next to our new medical supplies and one for the car.

Just in case.

12.

She Showed Up Anyway

I was on my way to pick up my aunt from the airport.

Auntie Bonnie, my godmother, my dad's sister and my lifeline. She's been a part of my life since before I could speak. Throughout my life, she has held me when I couldn't hold myself. She saw me when I couldn't see anything but loss. She was one of the few people who didn't try to fix me years ago.

She stayed steady.
She stayed softhearted.
She stayed tall, even at five foot one.

Growing up, my dad used to say, "You're so much like your Aunt Bonnie sometimes." I didn't ask what he meant. It didn't matter really. I just took it as a compliment.

She believes in people with her whole heart. She doesn't back down when she cares about something or someone. She wears her emotions openly and she's never once asked me to shrink mine.

I had called her before the hurricane hit. She didn't offer advice or warnings, she just listened. She said, "I trust you." Not in a performative way, just genuine, grounded trust.

She told me she knew I'd already thought everything through. She didn't doubt me for a second. "Just let me know when to come," she said. She was already packed and waiting, over a thousand miles away. She offered to fly down and sleep in a rental car in the driveway. If that's what it took to be close to us.

And she meant it.

When I got to the airport, I was pacing. I switched sides of the terminal every time a tram arrived, scanning the faces stepping through the glass doors, searching for her. I must have switched sides a half dozen times before I finally saw her and when I did, I ran.

She smiled like she'd been waiting a lifetime to be right where she was. We hugged like something in me had been reassembled just by the fact that she showed up. Her suitcase was full of art supplies, little gifts, and activities for the kids. She had packed intention into every zippered pocket.

I was so disoriented when I had arrived at the airport, a place I usually navigate effortlessly, that I parked in the farthest section. A parking lot I hadn't even known existed because of its inconvenient location. I apologized for the walk. She didn't care.

"We're wandering together," she said.

Over the course of her visit, she slipped into the spaces we didn't know how to fill. She helped with errands, with cooking, with the laundry piling up behind our panic. She moved through the rental like someone who already knew where everything belonged.

Greg had already gone back to work, setting up in a corner of the rental bedroom for full days of virtual meetings. I was back at the house during the day shoveling muck, rearranging fans, cataloging loss after loss. She took care of everything in between. She didn't need to ask what we needed, she just saw it.

With the kids, she didn't hover. She didn't push advice or guidance.

She just stayed present.

Fay clung to her from the moment she arrived. She needed the security of a grown-up wrapped in the costume of play. They made a cardboard cash register together and opened an imaginary store. Fay gave lessons on supply and demand, inventing a pricing system that fluctuated based on foot traffic and glitter availability. They hummed songs while sculpting tiny Play-Doh groceries. Fay's voice was lighter that week, still fragile, but lighter.

Landon needed something else. He needed space for recovery without a spotlight. She gave him what he needed. She let him zone out when he needed to and when he came around, when he felt like joining, she made space for him too. He helped plan meals, brainstormed ideas, and participated in their craft circle. Quietly, but present.

She held both kids in exactly the way they needed. No pressure. No expectations. Just unwavering availability.

But a few days in, the forecasts shifted. When the weight of everything started to settle, the announcement came.

Hurricane Milton.

Another storm.
What they were calling a potential superstorm.
A category 5.

Another chance to lose everything we were barely managing to hold.

We were still mopping the last of the muck from our floors. Still dragging ruined memories to the street. And still trying to convince ourselves we were moving forward. Now we had to prepare again but with dwindling supplies, gutted stores, and exhausted hands.

The anxiety didn't slam into me all at once. It seeped in, slow and heavy, pooling behind my ribs. *What happens to the debris on our front lawn, if another storm comes? How can we survive another blow when we're already sinking? What's left to lose that hasn't already been taken?*

I tried to be steady. Tried to pull the brave face on like a mask but I could feel the cracks running under my skin. We were still navigating the immediate aftermath of Helene. We had survived on adrenaline, on the delusion of it almost being over. What if it was just beginning? Another storm coming right at us. Larger. Stronger. Unbelievable.

Auntie Bonnie hadn't even been here a week yet. We were just beginning to breathe again and now I had to ask her to leave. I hated making the call. *I had promised myself I wouldn't.*

I told myself, she had earned the right to stay through whatever came next.

But love doesn't guarantee safety.

Not here.
Not anymore.

I needed her to be somewhere she could be protected. Somewhere dry. Somewhere outside the zone. I couldn't risk her getting stuck here or worse... I didn't want to have to explain to her husband and children why she didn't make it home.

She didn't argue. Of course she didn't. She understood in the way only someone who's carried difficult decisions can. She packed. The kids set up a goodbye picnic outside for lunch. She performed a last handful of skits with the kids in the living room. We all laughed until our stomachs ached. Then I loaded her bags into my car and brought her to the airport.

Some kinds of heartbreak are preventative.
You carry them early, so you don't have to carry something worse later.

This wasn't just about broken houses anymore.
It was about knowing when to let go.
Knowing when love means asking someone to walk away.
Knowing when survival demands you stand alone again.

Even if every bone in your body is begging not to.

13.

Hands, Masks, and Muck

Sometime in the first 72 hours since we laid eyes on our home again, I posted to the "Handy Women" Facebook group. I was still trying to process what had happened and still running on pure survival reflex.

"How do I lift a fridge that's fallen over?" It sounded ridiculous, even as I typed it. I had just posted a few weeks earlier, showing off the restoration projects I was so proud of.

Now, I was posting photos of it all destroyed. I wasn't expecting much. Maybe a few comments. Maybe some advice about straps or crowbars.

Instead, the messages poured in.

Women from all over Florida who were strangers to me, offering to drive across counties, hours out of their way, just to show up and help lift a fridge. And then, when they found out about the rest, the soaked walls, the ruined furniture, the entire hollowed-out house, they came to do more than lift.

They came to carry it with us.

Within hours, one of the Handy Women, Gisele, pulled into my driveway with a group of strangers from a local "Food Forest" gardening group.

They came inside without hesitation. Stepping through the slippery still mud covered floors, navigating through the sodden air. They carried out ruined mattresses and area rugs, twisted furniture, and wheelbarrows loaded with our life shredded by water.

More came over the next few days. Some volunteers traveling from as far as Deltona, across the state. Women I had never met, giving up their weekends and days off, to sweat and haul and clean for people they didn't even know.

They didn't need a reason bigger than this:
They had been through it once too, or they hadn't, but just couldn't bear to sit still while someone else was.

It felt like standing in the middle of a burning building and having strangers form a human chain through the flames. No questions asked. No pleading to be saved required.

A family friend sent her son and his friends to help too. She had just sent her cousin the week before. They drove over an hour, unloaded the storage container, carried salvageable bins into the remains of the house. They joked and tried to lighten the mood. I laughed along, until someone asked about the kids.

Our kids.

"How are they doing?" One of them politely inquired. I could feel the words snag in my throat as I tried to reply. I don't remember exactly what I said. I just remember the sudden, awful lump in my throat. The sting behind my eyes. The way I tried to stay composed but felt myself unraveling right there in the sun.

I excused myself and walked quickly around the side of the house, pretending to check something. *Pretending I had control.* I leaned against the muddy siding still covered in plastic. Then I slid down it, my legs buckling underneath me, until I was crouched low in a pile of hot gravel.

The cry which broke out of me wasn't quiet.
It was violent.
Primal.

A body-deep kind of sorrow clawed its way out no matter how hard I pressed my hands over my own mouth.

Sobbing so hard my chest ached, my fingers shaking as I tried to wipe away the tears and the snot and the shame. I didn't want anyone to see. I didn't want to make it anyone else's burden. So after a while, I cleaned myself up. I stood up straight. I wiped my face until it was passable. I walked back around the house and rejoined the work like nothing had happened, hoping no one had noticed.

Just another broken piece.
Just another thing to patch over until it could hold again.

***

About three weeks after the flood, another team showed up. They were volunteers from a nonprofit disaster relief group I had reached out to. Ten people. Organized. Efficient. Led by a retired general contractor who could direct a room full of chaos like he was conducting an orchestra. They ripped out more drywall, tore up trim and heavy soaked insulation. Cleared mountains of debris with calm expertise.

At one point, I overheard someone cursing about how hard it was to remove the drywall corner beads. I peeked my head around the corner, grinning sheepishly.

"Sorry," I said. "That was me. I really wanted to make sure everything was installed securely." We all laughed loudly, honestly and through the exhaustion.

Even destruction couldn't completely erase the stubborn pride I had in what we had built.

The help was overwhelming.
Incredible.
Humbling.

We were so grateful. *It saved us in ways I still don't know how to explain with precision.*

But the thing about triage is it's not meant to last.

They came, they lifted, they carried. They did what they came to do. Then they went home. Eventually they returned back to their cities, their families, their jobs, and their lives. They returned to the normal rhythms of the world and we were left standing in the remaining loss.

Alone again.

On what seemed like an island made of debris and water stains. Moving slower, heavier, stuck on a timeline the rest of the world wasn't following anymore.

The triage ended.
The loneliness began to grow.
The calls slowed down.

The attention drifted to the next disaster, the next emergency, the next story demanding a different kind of help. And we stayed here. Working in the ruined houses. On the gutted streets. Living a kind of life that may have looked normal from a distance, but up close was barely holding itself together.

While the rest of the world moved on.

14.

The Mercy Clause

While our staggered help from volunteers was taking place, the help took an abrupt pause as Hurricane Milton barreled towards us.

Everyone was preparing or pretending.
Or both.

The main street was completely gridlocked now with people trying to flee. Frantic evacuations, bumper to bumper. *The logic of panic.*

I watched them from the shoulder lane, stuck in my own kind of traffic. Part of me wanted to join them. The other part, wanted to watch the storm finish the job of the ones before.

I kept hoping something would hit our house.

Not in a destructive way, not exactly. But maybe a tree would crash through the roof and solve it all for us. Maybe the wind would drag the whole mess into the Gulf and we'd finally be eligible for help that meant something. *I know how that sounds.* But when every form of survival costs more than starting over, the idea of devastation begins to look like a kind of mercy.

Our home was barely a healed wound before Helene.
Then Mother Nature decided to tear it back open.

She poured salt from the river into its flesh.

A stinging reminder that we didn't belong here.
But didn't she know we were trying to leave?

We wished she had taken the skeleton too.

Which is ironic because before the hurricanes that damaged our home, we had paid to prevent this exact scenario I was now hoping for. We had removed the dead trees before Idalia was even a prediction. We had replaced the roof too, with the expensive fancy underlayment and all. We had tried to be responsible. To be smart. To protect the house we were now hoping might collapse.

Now, our responsibility had made us ineligible.

I used to think if your house flooded during a hurricane, surely it would also count as wind damage.

How could it not?

How could a storm rip through our town with enough force to shove water over two feet up our interior walls, but somehow leave us without a single penny of homeowner's coverage?

There's a trick to it, I told myself the second time. Flood damage and wind damage are two different kingdoms.

Homeowner's insurance governs what comes through your home: wind-broken windows, fallen trees, flying debris, roof leaks. Flood insurance governs what comes from the ground up.

We had already opened a homeowner's claim after Helene. I knew they probably wouldn't cover anything but I was trying to hold out hope. They sent out an inspector. He found just under $600 of wind damage. The hurricane deductible was $5,000. So they denied it. We weren't expecting a windfall, just hoping for a crack in the wall.

Something. Anything. Maybe some roof shingles out of place and a few soffits pulled free. Maybe a leak or evidence of the house shifting from pressure that meant it was now compromised enough.

Just enough to qualify us for "Loss of Use" coverage.
Just enough to qualify for help with lodging.
Just enough of a claim it could be an additional safety net for what lay ahead.

But the roof held.
The deductible stood.
And we were on our own again.

Still, I had filed the flood insurance claim after we evacuated. Before we even returned to see the damage ourselves. I didn't wait. I knew what we'd find.

When the flood adjuster finally called to schedule the inspection, I told him I was already working on our personal property spreadsheet. That I'd have it sent over before he ever took a step into our house to view the damage. He paused then said, "If you actually do that, it'll be a first for me. No one has it ready by the time I show up." I told him this wasn't my first rodeo. Let him know we had flooded last year. I was going to use what I learned. I was going to help him expedite the claim.

And I did.

I finished the spreadsheet, room by room, line by line. Built a folder of evidence: photos, receipts, serial numbers, replacement values. I sent it with plenty of time to spare before he was scheduled to make it to our area. Then the inspection was delayed.

We got pushed to the back of his claim queue.

It didn't matter that I'd been fast. It didn't matter how thorough I was. It didn't matter, I had done everything they tell you to do.

The system wasn't designed to reward you.
It was designed to wait you out.
To make you repeat yourself.
To make you doubt what you already lived through.

***

We gathered our supplies and waited out the newest storm in the rental. *We were trying to act like we weren't scared.*

Like the layers of experience had built enough armor to keep us from flinching. But even the cat was hunkered down, his body low and stiff. The kids wrapped themselves in blankets and stared at the TV like it was a shield. Greg and I glued to our phones waiting for the latest updates.

Milton came and went.
We were "spared."

This time, it wasn't our neighborhood. Other places nearby were hit harder. Neighborhoods who had made it through Helene were shredded by Milton. Roofs torn. Trees through windows. Power lines tangled like vines.

The damage was spreading even wider now. Less predictable. Hurricanes had started taking turns with different zip codes.

Milton had passed, but the gas shortages were getting worse. I started canvassing gas stations on my drives between the rental and our house. Watching. Documenting. Hoping. I'd text neighbors whenever I spotted a delivery. I would make quick announcements so they could fuel their generators before the pumps were dry again. Some stations were already wrapped in plastic like corpses. Saran Wrap over the nozzles meant no gas, no hope, no point.

Generators mean nothing without gas. Gas means nothing if you can't find it. Store shelves became increasingly emptied and there was already a county-wide curfew in place.

But we didn't worry about looters this time. There was nothing left worth stealing. I joked that if someone did break in, they'd better take some of the debris with them. *The least they could do was help us clean up.* Even our personal losses were just a reflection of something larger.

Something orchestrated.

Insurance in Florida isn't just a risk calculation anymore.

It's a controlled retreat. Companies pulling out. Policies dropped with no warning. Underwriters vanishing. Fewer options means less competition. And less competition means no incentive to keep things fair.

Only profitable.

They call it a market correction, as if it's neutral. As if it's gravity. But this isn't gravity. It's math with a motive.

And when disaster strikes, they don't show up with resources. Instead, they show up with adjusters. With loopholes. With loss limits. With denials wrapped in polite phrases like "peril not covered." *They don't show up with relief.* They show up with paperwork then make you wait.

It's not just broken, I keep telling myself.
It's functioning exactly as intended.

The insurance CEOs are still making huge amounts of recorded profit.

We're not protected.
We're profiled.

Even as the risk of being affected by hurricanes continues to spread to states and areas that once seemed safe.

AFTERMATH (BY THE NUMBERS)

Hurricane Idalia
August 2023
Category 3 at landfall
Estimated damages cost: $3.6 billion
Recorded deaths: 5

Hurricane Helene
September 2024
Category 4 with sustained winds of 140 MPH
Estimated damages cost: $78.7 billion
Recorded deaths: 219

Hurricane Milton
October 2024
At its peak before landfall Milton was a category 5 with sustained winds of 180 MPH
Downgraded to Category 3 with sustained winds of 120 MPH at landfall
Estimated damages cost: up to $34.3 billion
Recorded deaths: 32

These are only the hurricanes I reference in this book.

The total cost of U.S. billion-dollar disasters over the last 5 years (2020-2024) is $746.7 billion* (cited statistics from climate.gov and noaa.gov)

These numbers measure recorded loss ratios and wind speed.
They calculate estimated monetary value.

They don't count how many of my neighbors are still sitting on their flooded couches. They don't count people without formal housing and paperwork to back their claim. They don't count the grandparents who lost their homes but won't say a word because they don't want to be a burden. *They don't count what doesn't meet the criteria to qualify.*

They don't count relationships unraveling in hot rooms. Or the people crying in their cars so no one sees them. They don't count missed milestones of loved ones now gone.

They don't include enough room for the collective us.
The lives beyond statistics.

Yes, I'm in there somewhere.
But not really.

15.

Your Story Moved Us

We were already drowning in logistics. I didn't think anyone was paying attention. Then the phone rang and I remembered what it felt like to be seen before you're ready.

I hadn't gone inside yet. I was still clean, or clean enough. A folded change of clothes sat beside me on the passenger seat. There was a breakfast shake sweating in the cupholder. A new box of contractor bags lay unopened on the floor behind me, like I could still pretend none of this would require them.

I sat in the driver's seat, engine off, hands loose in my lap, staring at the house. I wasn't frozen but I wasn't ready. Not for the smell or the humidity. Not for the feeling that I'd already done all this once, and still somehow had to do it again.

Then my phone rang. It was from an unknown number, which at the time, could have been anything or anyone. It could have been insurance, FEMA, a contractor, a volunteer. Someone with help or maybe questions, needing me to explain my life again by filling out lines in a form.

I answered because I couldn't afford not to these days.

His voice was measured. Practiced, but kind. He said he was calling from the company GoFundMe. For a moment, I worried I had done something wrong. Like maybe I'd violated an unwritten rule about

83

how desperate you're allowed to sound. Maybe I selected the wrong option and they were shutting the fundraiser down.

Instead, he said he'd read our fundraiser page.

"Your story moved us," he said.
"We'd like to amplify it."

I blinked. The house sat silent in front of me. The breakfast shake remained unopened. "If any media reached out," he continued, "would you be willing to talk with them?" I said yes. I didn't even pause because exposure meant possible help. Help meant momentum and momentum meant maybe we'd get out before the next flood hit, *whenever that might be.*

I hadn't wanted to make the fundraiser at all. I hovered over the "publish" button for what felt like days. Not because I thought we didn't deserve help but because I wasn't sure anyone would agree. I wrote it like a tightrope, not too dramatic, not too vague. Just factual enough to be believed, and just emotional enough to be human. I hated how careful I had to be. How much it felt like marketing our survival. But we were rationing plans like groceries, so I clicked "publish" and closed the tab. And braced for judgment.

I didn't know what "amplify it" was really going to mean for us. I just waited to see if something would happen.

Over a week later, another unknown number.

Same reflex. This time, a reporter from a national news syndicate. He said he was writing a story about hurricane recovery, fake stories spreading around the internet and the role online fundraisers like GoFundMe played with helping families move forward. He'd seen ours and wanted to talk. He said it would be a quick call, maybe fifteen, twenty minutes. We stayed on the phone for almost an hour.

I told him everything. The floods, last year's repairs, the help we were receiving and the GoFundMe. I told him about the insurance systems seemingly pretending to care but how they make you repeat your suffering for proof. I told him about the FEMA representative from last year. How she had gone through Katrina, and that's why she decided to join FEMA years ago.

I explained how much it meant to be helped by someone who knew what we were going through. *Someone who got it.*

I told him I was afraid misinformation could impact the safety of people like her. The ones just trying to do their jobs. The ones that were there to help in the ways they could. I believe the program is important. It's not wrong to want to improve these systems but there is a difference between critique and just wanting to eliminate it all together.

He asked thoughtful questions. He listened.

Then he asked:
"What does your husband do for work?"

I paused.

"Can I tell you off the record?" I asked.
"This story is mine. I don't want to complicate things for him."

He agreed.

I told him Greg was a federal employee. His job wasn't political but nuance doesn't always matter. I wanted that part of our life kept out of anything public. Even though his role had nothing to do with FEMA, it didn't feel safe to be visible. Not in an election year. Not when FEMA had become a flashpoint in a political firestorm.

Technically, whoever won the presidency would be Greg's new boss.

Not in his most direct chain of command, but at the top. You don't want visibility during a corporate merger. It was like that. *It wasn't censorship, it was a form of self-preservation.*

This wasn't my first time speaking with the media. Over the years, I'd been interviewed for news stories, quoted in opinion pieces, even featured in a national video series for my advocacy initiatives. I knew how this worked. I knew how framing could shift a message. How nuance could vanish in the editing room. And how the human parts could get reduced to a headline built for traction.

I went into the interview cautious, deliberate, and clear. I thought if I was careful, if I told the truth cleanly enough, the story would reflect that. But it still landed differently than I expected. Not because I said the wrong thing but because you can't fit an hour long conversation into a single news article.

A few days later, the article came out. There it was, my name, my story, a few quotes and a photo. The headline was about conspiracy theories and politics. I understood the angle and the article was well written. It didn't matter though, my stomach dropped anyway. I had just shared what was true to me, but I felt like I'd been pulled into something bigger than me and not in a good way.

What if someone at Greg's job saw it? What if it made him look reckless or disloyal, just by association?

No one silenced me but I started editing myself in a new way. Not because I didn't have something to say.

I did. I always have.

If we were possibly going to face consequences anyway, I would've given them my whole dissertation on bureaucracy. On propaganda. On the way these systems grind people down and divide the rest while masquerading as politics.

I wanted to tell him that disaster survivors from all political backgrounds were facing these same insurance denials. The same bureaucratic maze. This wasn't about red or blue, but about systems failing all of us.

But that wasn't what the news story was supposed to be about. And the cost of going off script wasn't just mine to pay, so it changed the calculation.

So instead of shouting, I whispered "Please pay attention."
Instead of "Why does this even need to be said?" It became "I hope someone notices anyway."

The guilt over deciding to speak, didn't come alone. It arrived beside another feeling, something between shame and confusion.

Why had GoFundMe picked us?
Why had the reporter called me?

I had actually asked these questions out loud to them. Their responses seemed to make sense at the time. But I just kept thinking to myself about how our home wasn't ripped from its foundation. We weren't rescued by helicopter. We weren't missing.

We were just... here. Treading.

In the weeks following Hurricane Helene, I read story after story from North Carolina. Entire families were swept away. Homes buried by landslides. Communities erased. And all I could think was, *why us?*

I felt gross about it.

Here I am, upset my kids have to live through this again...
They GET TO LIVE through this because they are alive.
We get to live through this again because we are all alive.

...Not everyone has that chance.

There are people dead. People missing. People much worse off than us.

Water didn't reach my ceilings. My husband still had a job. We still had a functioning car and for all intents and purposes our house technically was still standing.

Why did I get to speak?

It's a strange thing, being chosen for sympathy.
There's a weight to it.
Like if you're being seen, you better justify the gaze.

So I started revising myself before anyone else could. I didn't stop speaking but I stopped feeling like the story was mine. I watched my own mouth every time I opened it. I never stopped worrying about who I could hurt or who I was overshadowing. I never stopped wondering who might be listening, and what it might cost our family if they were.

I still had something to say. I just needed to learn how to say it safely.

16.

Accepting Help

Weeks after the volunteers left, I found myself delivering water and cleaning supplies to neighbors who still hadn't asked for help.

The line for supplies stretched farther than I had expected. We waited in a snake of cars baking under the relentless sun, wrapped tight around the block. I sat behind the wheel, sweat sliding down my back, but I barely felt it anymore. The heat, the exhaustion, they had become part of me, like the dust in the air and the pressure in my chest.

My neighbor Lori sat beside me. She was here for herself and Steve, sure. But I was the one who had insisted we come.

"We'll pick up extras," I'd said.
"For the neighbors."

Last year, after the first hurricane, we told ourselves we didn't need charity because others had it worse. Because we were strong enough to recover and rebuild alone. I wore the decision like armor. Told myself it was about pride, self-sufficiency, but standing in line now, inching forward, I knew better.

This wasn't about pride.
It wasn't even about strength.
It was about survival.

Survival doesn't care about dignity.
It doesn't care how much you gave.
It only cares if you're still breathing.

I gripped the steering wheel, my fingers slipping on the worn leather.
The truth settled in my stomach.

You can survive alone.
I had.
But it carves something out of you.

Accepting help wasn't new to me, technically. I let the volunteers haul out wreckage and clear debris we couldn't carry alone. *I let them.* Smiled stiffly. Said thank you too many times. I tried not to crumble under the shame prickling under my skin. I thought letting them help would be enough but here I was again stuck in another moment of asking. A part of me still hated it.

When we finally reached the front, a volunteer handed us bottled water, cleaning supplies, and MREs. I stared at the stack in my lap.

MREs. Meals Ready to Eat.

I had never seen MREs this up close before, I held them in my hands examining them. *Aren't those for people who've lost everything? People who are truly desperate? Were we really in that situation now? Are we those people now?*

The thought stuck in my throat. I swallowed hard. Looking around, it was obvious. We were. We had crossed an invisible line without even realizing it.

The volunteer asked if I had children.

A simple question. Routine. But it hit like a body blow.
"Yes," I croaked. "Two kids."

Just saying it made my skin itch, like I'd confessed something shameful. It wasn't just the asking, it was the admitting that we were in a place where we couldn't make it on our own. I feared judgment. It wasn't just about feeding them. It was also about everything they didn't know they had lost. The life we had promised them. A life safe, steady, and whole.

Yet somehow I had put them in this line, even if they weren't in the car with me.

I kept telling myself:
This isn't forever.
Just right now.

But the voice felt thin.
Tired.
Like a radio signal barely coming through.

Maybe helping others was the only reason I could accept help at all. Wrapping it up in someone else's needs made it feel less like failure. It didn't feel good. It didn't erase the ache in my chest. But it made it bearable.

I thought about the women I'd supported over the years. The other assault survivors who sat shaking across from me. I'd told them to ask for help.

"Let people in," I used to say.
"Let them carry a little of it with you."

And yet here I was, on the other side of my own advice, learning just how hard it was to live what I preached. It's easier to give than to need. Easier to be the hand pulling someone out of the wreckage.

Needing feels too much like drowning.

But survival reshapes you. It stretches you. Especially when you've stitched yourself back together with shaking hands.

I think that's why I had thrown myself into advocacy and into disaster response because I knew what it cost to survive alone. I preached community, like gospel. I built spaces where others could fall apart without shame. Yet even after everything, I rarely stepped onto those bridges myself. *Not without first proving I deserved to be there.* Maybe that's why sitting in line, accepting those supplies, felt like surrender. *Not to weakness, but to the truth.*

Survival isn't supposed to be a solitary act.
And maybe belonging isn't something you always have to earn.

It wasn't just about the supplies, it was about accepting the reality of our situation. It was about accepting the fact that we were part of something bigger than ourselves. I didn't want to be someone who needed help.

But I was.
We were.

***

I went back to the distribution center a second time a couple weeks later. This time, we parked and walked inside. I brought Steve with me. He didn't say much as we crossed the threshold, but I could feel the weight in his steps. We weren't there to stock up. We were there because we needed to be.

A volunteer stopped us at the door and asked for our address. Wanted to know if we were really victims of the hurricane. Wanted proof we belonged here.

I blinked. Not because I didn't have the words but because I hadn't expected to be doubted. I told him our street, the flood line, what we'd lost. Another worker overheard. Someone who knew me. She stepped in, confirmed my story. The first man's shoulders eased.

"Sorry," he said, voice low. "We've had a few people trying to take advantage. Our cameras are down and donations have gone missing. Full pallets of tarps, food and tools have disappeared. We've even had people showing up claiming to be storm victims, but we are pretty sure they were contractors, laborers, folks looking for a free score."

He wasn't cold. Just tired. Suspicious in the way people become after too many betrayals.

We went inside, gathered what we needed, basic supplies. Toiletries, shelf-stable food, paper goods, rakes, shovels and more cleaning products. Even though we were back in the car within twenty minutes, I couldn't stop thinking about what the man had said.

About the ones who weren't victims. The ones who pretended to be.

Who the hell steals supplies meant for people who can't afford to patch a leaking roof?

It wasn't just wrong, it was a theft of trust, humanity and dignity. Every stolen tarp and every hoarded box of donated food meant another barrier for someone like me. Someone who already had to swallow their pride just to walk through the door.

Disaster shouldn't have to come with suspicion but it often does. It turns every act of asking into something heavier than it should be.

After I dropped Steve off, I sorted through the supplies, gathered extras from inside the house, and headed back down the street. I pulled into another neighbor's driveway, careful not to crush the scattered debris. I approached their motorhome and called out:

"Hey, it's Ashley! I wanted to drop off a few things."

I opened my trunk and started unloading. I've learned some people won't ask for what they need either. They will only accept it, if refusing seems rude. But I knew they needed help. This retired couple, living on a fixed income in their driveway after their house was taken by the water too. They hadn't flooded last year and hoped they'd be spared again. But water doesn't care if you've paid your dues. It doesn't care if you're almost 70 and can't afford to start over.

They accepted my help again, quietly wishing they could afford to be too proud. I handed them information on other resources I knew they'd probably never call. They were too weary and afraid after past promises of assistance turned into scams.

Why do we live in a world where the most vulnerable fear the cost of accepting help?

I don't have the answer.
But I've made peace with being the trusted exception. If I can be that for them, a small lifeline, I will. I already knew I'd be back.

I'll be damned if I let the world forget them.

I head to the next house.
Arms full and determined.

17.

Through My Son's Eyes

I've tried not to represent my children. I've tried to let them have their own memories. Their own grief. Their own timelines. But this story isn't mine alone. And some things, they've already begun putting into words.

What follows is an unedited essay Landon (12 years old) wrote about what it felt like to walk back into our house a few weeks after the second flood. His voice is different from mine. More straightforward. More honest in some ways. He doesn't try to explain what it meant. He just tells you what he saw. He wanted to share his point of view with you.

He wants to be heard too.
So I'm letting him speak for himself.

"We pulled into the driveway of our house. It wasn't the first time we had been back to the house after a flood but I still didn't feel used to seeing it like this. It seemed normal... at first, but there was still mud on the sidewalk and the outside felt a little more off than usual, but I couldn't pinpoint why. Dad had us put on gloves and a mask before entering. As I walked into the house for the first time after Hurricane Helene I was in shock as every wall was completely destroyed already. There was damage everywhere. Drywall all over the floors mud all around the trim... you name it.

This wasn't the house's original state. Mom and dad and some volunteers had already been gutting the house for the last couple of weeks. It had been cleaned out for the most part but there was still dirt, grime, and broken pieces EVERYWHERE. Last year Fay and I didn't return to the house for almost a month after the flood so we never saw it fully like this soon after the storm. By the time I got to my room I felt a disturbing feeling even before fully entering the room. First off there wasn't a door to enter through but then I stepped inside and fully saw it.

Or maybe it was what I didn't see that hit me first. My bed was gone, my closet was torn into pieces, all my belongings that used to fill my room were all gone. It was my room but it didn't quite feel like it anymore. I turned to the side and I realized the wall that separated my room from the bathroom was gone. I was staring right through to the toilet, where the sink used to be and a still mud covered tub.

Mom gathered some tools and dad found a place to start and we got to work. Mom said we could take out our anger on the walls that betrayed us so that is what we did. Fay grabbed a sledgehammer and I grabbed a crowbar and we started demolishing everything we could under the 4 foot mark. Mom showed me how to kick in a wall "properly." I stood up straight and lifted my leg backwards to get some momentum and kicked forward with the sole of my boot. It felt pretty good, exquisite almost. I could feel a rush of satisfaction as I loosened giant chunks of wall much more than I could have done with a hammer.

When we finished for the day I washed my hands outside with the hose but really I was still dirty. I went back inside and started searching for my possessions to see what had been saved. Luckily for me, most of my favorite belongings survived. They were safe up in the loft, packed away in bags and boxes. More of my things were saved this time than last year. Mom was still taking pictures of everything for insurance. I didn't want to record any of it because I didn't want to have to remember more than I already will.

Last year was hard and it took a really long time to feel normal again. This time being the second flood I knew it could be just as difficult but it already felt different. I didn't feel as hopeless, I wasn't as surprised or devastated... I didn't really feel anything at all."

I never wanted him to know how to kick down drywall.
But I'm proud he learned how.

18.

The House Across the Street

A month after Helene, our neighbors Steve and Lori still hadn't asked for help with their house. They had avoided having to ask last year and still hadn't reached out this time around.

They have been a constant since the day that we moved into the neighborhood.

Through every inconsistency, every storm, every moment of doubt, they were there. They were the very first people to greet us, helping us unload our moving truck without hesitation. From that moment on, they became part of our everyday life.

Steve is a retired dock worker and Lori is a retired school bus driver. They have taught our kids to fish. They baked banana bread for birthdays, decorated together with us for holidays, and showed up to celebrate every achievement. They sat with us to mourn losses. Even the quiet ones, like the death of pets. *They aren't just neighbors.*

When our home flooded last year from Idalia, they insisted on helping.

Steve paused his own repairs to make sure our kids had safe, drywalled rooms to return to. He gave us his time, his tools, his steadiness. He became my second set of hands and my sounding board. Offering construction tips from a lifetime of experience. He helped me refine my skills and keep my head above water. *Steve helped repair half of our neighborhood last year yet they never asked for anything in return.*

So when another hurricane had hit and I saw the exhaustion in their faces, I knew I needed to step in. Even if they wouldn't admit they needed help. Even if they would never ask for it. This time, they needed someone to do for them what they'd done for us.

They had stayed during the storm, trying to protect their home. The floodwaters still found a way in. They were the ones who had the eel swimming through their living room. Both of their vehicles were flooded. One had already been towed away, the other sat in their garage with towels on top of the wet seats and plastic over the windows which would no longer close.

And they needed someone to step in before they fell even further. Lori had already literally fallen. She slipped in the mud just after the storm and hadn't been the same since. When I came over, she was sitting on their still-damp, mold-ridden couch, in a home that no longer felt like a home.

I went out and found her a walker.

I had brought them to the local donation hub. Steve's face lit up when he spotted cans of Chef Boyardee ravioli, his favorite. It was such a small thing, but the joy on his face was unmistakable.

Later, I told Danette about that moment. She was a volunteer I had just connected with a few days prior. She'd been cooking hot meals for hurricane victims in our area with help from her visiting mother. Normally, she prepared large trays of baked ziti. Easy to scale and easy to deliver but after hearing about Steve's ravioli moment, she changed the menu.

That night, she made ravioli,
just for them.

When the meal arrived, it was more than food. It was dignity, wrapped in foil and kindness. You taste things differently when they're made with love. When they show up in a moment you thought you'd been forgotten. Danette made and distributed over 100 meal trays to hurricane victims. She filled hearts and stomachs all across our county.

In the same week, I met Rachel, who brought a friend and a truck full of tools to Steve and Lori's home. I found her in a hurricane help group online while searching for assistance for my neighbors.

After finishing my day's work on my own gutted house, I threw on a fresh pair of gloves and new facemask. Then walked across the street with extra gear. Together, we got to work, cutting breakaway lines in the drywall, tearing out soaked insulation, clearing mold, sweeping, and vacuuming. It wasn't dramatic, but it was hard work and it mattered.

During a much needed break, Rachel asked how I was doing. I gave her my practiced answer... the one I'd already used a dozen times that week. "It just is what it is." "We are just doing what needs to be done" "We are handling it one day at a time."

She saw right through it. She didn't press, but she acknowledged it. She didn't look away.

She told me about another couple she'd helped. A family who'd lost their child years ago. Now the flood had taken the last of their keepsakes. Her voice softened. Every family, she said, has a different story... but the grief? That part was universal. Rachel ended up physically helping a total of 125 households damaged by the storms, over the course of this year. She had a deep understanding of what she was talking about.

She didn't know it yet , but she gave me something that day.

She reminded me there were people capable of seeing me. Not just the work. Not just the survival. Me. Beneath the composure. Beneath the strength. Beneath the answers.

And in doing so, she forced me to continue to confront the affliction I was still carrying. The heartache of always being the one who helps. The quiet question that kept surfacing, of whether people could show up the way I show up for others.

But she did.
And Danette did.
And Steve and Lori already had.

Their effort didn't feel like luck.
It didn't feel like an anomaly.
And that made a difference.

Steve and Lori didn't think people would care. They thought their window for help from others had closed. They assumed they were too late to qualify, too isolated and too overlooked. They didn't think people would still want to show up for them but they were wrong.

I'm so grateful I got to prove them wrong. They had given so much to our community, to our family, and to our little street. It was time someone gave back to them.

Because no one, no one, should have to sit on a mold-covered couch, in pain, and wonder if their life still matters to the people around them.

Especially not when they've spent so much of their own life showing up for others.

This time, we showed up for them.

19

No Room for Tornadoes

Almost a month after moving into our first rental, we were packing again.

Another short-term rental. No permanent address. Just another GPS coordinate marked as our current parking spot. Another unfamiliar place to try to sleep. Another house we'd pretend to live in.

While filling our bags, I could feel the resistance in my body before I knew why. My hands worked fast, sorting, gathering, rolling towels into shape, but my chest stayed tight.

I didn't want to separate, not even for a few hours.
Even if to make the move easier.

And that's when it hit me. I wasn't in this rental house anymore.
Mentally, I was in last year's.

After Idalia, we'd moved into another rental, barely recovered. We were still processing the flood, the insurance calls, the first version of letting go. The day we transitioned between the two rentals, I had a virtual therapy appointment. It was the only piece of support I had managed to schedule for myself in weeks. I told Greg he could take the kids and go pick up the rest of our belongings, including our food still being stored in the other rental's kitchen.

I suggested they go without me, so they didn't need to rush back for

103

my appointment. They agreed and took the car, while I stayed behind.

Alone.

That decision changed something in me.

The sky darkened while I sat in the new rental house, waiting for my therapist to join the session. Storm clouds moved fast. Alerts began pinging in rapid succession. Then the power cut out. And the signal dropped.

Three tornadoes.

One came within a mile of the Airbnb I was in. The gutters ripped off the house and flew across the yard like loose shrapnel. Rain hit the windows sideways. The air had an eerie weight to it. Subtle but wrong. Everything slows down just before it hits. I moved into the closet. A small flashlight in one hand, my phone in the other. Minimal food. Limited contact with my family.

I sat in the dark for four hours. Listening to the wind. Checking my phone for bars. Waiting to hear if another tornado was coming, or if I was just sitting still for nothing.

There is a very specific fear that comes when you're afraid of dying in a house which isn't yours. When you're afraid if you go missing, your husband will be left explaining to your children the difference between flooded and truly gone.

Greg and the kids were driving and had made it to a restaurant when the warnings came in. He didn't want to be on the road during the tornadoes. They waited there, crouched between booths with strangers and employees. Then, when it was clear they still couldn't get back to me. They had to change plans. They headed to the damaged home we owned... the one we had already lost to water.

They stayed there.

Since, somehow a broken house was safer than the lodging we were paying for. It was out of the danger zone and at least there was electricity and AC there.

I didn't know where they were for a while. My texts wouldn't send and my calls dropped mid-ring. The last message I'd gotten was about them trying to get back to me. Then came the silence, for what felt like forever.

I remember the sound the house made when the third storm cell passed overhead. The kind of sound which makes you stop breathing for a moment just to hear better. Like if you hold your breath, maybe the roof will too.

Afterwards, I stepped into the kitchen and into a puddle. My whole body seized. I thought the water had come again. Turns out the fridge had melted. The power loss had defrosted everything, and it leaked out in a quiet, creeping stream across the tile. I couldn't immediately identify it while navigating in the dark. Still, I cleaned it up. I laid down towels, emptied the melting ice tray into the sink and mopped the floor. I was trying to stop the puddle from warping their baseboards. I was protecting a house and it wasn't even mine.

Because that's what I do.
Even when I'm scared.
Even when I'm alone.

In total, I was stranded for eight hours. No food beyond crackers. Limited information. No real place to hide. Just me, the closet, the darkness and the wind.

When they finally got through the roadblocks and came back for me, I didn't fall apart. But I felt like a window left cracked during a storm. *Something had gotten in.*

***

Now, a year later, we were moving again. And my body remembered before I did. The way it tightened when Greg suggested he take a load ahead. The way I looked at our bags like they could betray me. I said no. We'd do it in shifts together. Even if it took twice as long. Even if it meant shoving everything into the car, using every inch of space. Even if we had to turn around three times for something we had forgotten or didn't have room for.

I wasn't going to be alone again.
Not like that.

We drove past the remnants of the tornadoes from last year. Some of the damage was still visible. Foundations exposed, blue tarps now bleached white by sun. You could see where whole blocks had pulled apart. The destruction from the tornadoes had cut sharper than the hurricanes. A reminder that just because you've already survived something doesn't mean worse can't find you.

Packing this time wasn't really about going somewhere new or even the transition of accommodations itself. It was about moving without splitting. It was about choosing togetherness over convenience.

Because survival doesn't always mean efficiency.

Sometimes it means refusing to be stranded again, even if no one thinks you should stay behind this time.

20.

Built Too Well

I don't know if this is grief or grout dust. It clings to my arms, coats my shirt, and creeps into my throat.

My hands ache but I keep working. I started with a chisel, crowbar and hammer. Prying at the backsplash one tile at a time. It wouldn't budge, not really. The tools slipped from the grout lines and off the ceramic tile like the wall was laughing at me. So I dropped the chisel and picked up the sledgehammer.

Not to restore anything.
Not to save what's left.

The tile cracked first. It felt like permission. Yet I was cursing myself for doing too thorough of a job attaching the tiles in the first place. Each one had been set tight to the cement board. No hollow voids, no gaps or weak points. I used to run my hand across this wall and feel proud. It was precise. *It was done right.*

But floodwaters don't care about craftsmanship. The storm surge had crept behind the seams I had sealed so carefully, making its way in from where the exterior walls met the foundation. They soaked the studs and hid behind the tile.

And stayed.

My work had held up so well that even now, with damage hiding behind it, I had to completely destroy it, tile by tile, just to let the walls breathe. This wasn't just demolition, it was an unmaking.

The sledgehammer was heavier than I remembered from the day before, and all the days before that. My arms burned with each swing. I chipped, swung, braced my feet, and did it again.

There are no doors left to buffer sound. The water took them too. They had swollen and splintered, sagged off their hinges, then finally gave out. We dragged them outside after the water receded. Mold had already bloomed in green, pink, and black, quicker than last year.

Now, the house echoes differently.

Harder.
More hollow.

There's nothing to muffle the clang of tile breaking or the breath I keep forgetting I'm holding. I don't bother with music anymore. I don't need distraction.

There's no illusion left to protect.

Just me, the sledgehammer, and the sound of something still alive inside these ruins I used to call home.

We're not rebuilding anything.
Not this time.

This house is a waiting room now. A holding pen for paperwork. It has become its own kind of purgatory. But I'm still here.

Still working.
Still alive.
Still making noise, even if it echoes now.

***

I wasn't always good at this. There was a time I flinched every time I pulled the trigger on a drill. When we first moved to Florida almost thirteen years ago, our starter home needed everything. The need for a full renovation, including a new roof, was how we could afford to buy it.

Greg had the training. He'd gone to trade school. I had little to no experience. He was the foreman, the crew, and the planner. I contributed in the ways I could. I tracked budgets, shopped for discounted materials, held flashlights and balanced boards. I was still learning the name of the tools I was retrieving for him.

I like to learn new things and I definitely don't like feeling useless.

So, I studied. I learned more than the names. I watched him, I asked questions, I researched materials, read how-tos, and started participating more than just assisting.

By the time our work schedules shifted, I had more time to work solo. I found something I never expected. I liked construction. I'd put on my headphones, block out the noise, and disappear into the geometry of it. Building became a language I understood. There was math in it, symmetry, and problem-solving. There was rhythm in leveling, pattern in trim, a kind of poetry in the precision. It was a kind of art in its own right, angular and stubborn and true.

The more confident I became, the more ambitious our projects grew. Custom built-ins and decorative moldings, upgrades we never could've financed without doing it ourselves. I started taking on entire projects from start to finish. Each one felt like a door opening.

***

Years earlier, when Landon was just a toddler, Greg and I had taken a weekend trip three hours north of where we used to live. Driving past Tampa, up the nature coast to the Big Bend of Florida. A town untouched by subdivisions and flocks of developers. Bursting with natural beauty and edged by rivers. Where the mermaids at Weeki Wachee swam near the springs full of manatees. We stayed in a tiny room, just a bed to crash in after full days exploring outside. We floated down a natural lazy river, and in that moment, we felt completely at peace.

We left with a dream.

After we got home, we pulled up real estate listings along the river we had floated down. It was out of reach, like fantasy-level unrealistic, but the seed was planted.

Years passed. When the heat swallowed our days and the ocean breeze disappeared, we would dream again of hypothetical moves back north. Still, winter always reminded us why we'd left and Florida always lured us to stay like a siren singing. When the humidity broke, when the coastal air returned, it whispered: *Remember why you came.*

So we stayed.

By the time our first house was almost completely renovated, the itch was back, and this time, we were ready to scratch it. One afternoon, while waiting for spackle to cure, I opened two tabs: one with comps for our current house, and another with listings up north.

Nothing fit.

Not the budget or the needed space. What we could afford in New England couldn't even be considered a reasonable trade-off.

So I opened a third tab. Just for fun. *What would it look like if we stayed in the South but somewhere different.* I searched all of Florida and parts of Georgia. Extra square footage, a garage, RV parking and garden space. Room to breathe and grow. I didn't expect anything to match. I didn't really think it was possible.

Then I saw it: a red dot on the map, hovering by a river. It was just outside the town we'd visited all those years ago. It had everything. It checked every unrealistic box while staying in our budget. It felt like a pipe dream turned real.

We should've known better.

But we didn't hesitate. The pictures showed age and wear, but also possibility. The house needed work, but we weren't scared. We were ready to put in the time and effort to make our dreams come true.

We called the owner. Within two weeks, we were walking the land. The dock was only 200 feet from the house. Gardens were ready to be expanded. We examined the inside of the house. We could visualize our life here. We imagined midday picnics by the water, turning the loft into the kids' playroom, setting up Greg's home office in the finished garage, turning the formal dining room into my sewing room.

We made an offer the next day.
Our tools were packed. We were going to make it ours.

***

Two and a half years later, I was swinging a sledgehammer at the same tile I had installed with my own hands. Once for the renovation and again after Hurricane Idalia and now for the third time, after Helene. I had left my job to renovate this house and to help us all transition into our new life when we moved here.

I never got to settle in.
And now I couldn't leave.
Each tile cracked, but still clung.

Just like us.

I used to think working with my hands meant control. If I measured twice, cut clean, and sealed tight, everything I loved would stay dry and sheltered.

But the water didn't ask permission. It found every angle I thought I'd closed. It made a mockery of my precision.

I had built too well and believed too hard.

Now all I can do is chip away at what I once called progress. One swing at a time.

21.

Borrowed Streets

We were still at our second short-term rental.

Another borrowed house.
Another set of unfamiliar walls trying to hold our lives together while
we caught our breath.

As I turned onto the quiet road, I spotted one of the neighbors outside.
A man, standing at the end of his driveway, watching the stillness settle
across the street. I slowed down, heart thudding harder than it should
have for something so small.

This was my chance.

Maybe he could tell me what I needed to know. Maybe he would let us
borrow a little belonging, even if it was only for one night.

I pulled into the driveway of the rental. The house that wasn't ours.
The house holding pieces of our life in bins and bags in corners we tried
not to look at too long.

I got out of the car. Still wearing the clothes I had been working in all
morning and afternoon. My pants stained with drywall dust, sweat
drying in patches across my back, the mark of someone trying to
rebuild faster than life could keep breaking.

I walked across the street, waving.

"Excuse me! Hi!" I called out, jogging the last few steps. "I'm staying in the rental across the street," I said, trying to sound casual, even as the words cracked slightly at the edges. "Do you mind me asking... does this street do trick-or-treating?" "We have two kids," I explained quickly.

"We lost our home to Hurricane Helene, and I just want them to be able to do something that feels normal." The words tumbled out faster than I intended, like if I said them fast enough, maybe they wouldn't sound so heavy.

He smiled, cautious at first, then warmer. He told me they had been watching us. His wife had seen me. Sneaking out before sunrise. Returning hours later carrying garbage bags into the rental. Moving like someone carrying not just belongings but something heavier.

She wasn't wrong. Every word of it was true.

I felt something knot in my stomach, not shame exactly, but the raw visibility survival usually tries to hide. They had seen us. Not just the moves, but the weight behind them. And they hadn't looked away.

He told me their little street didn't do much for Halloween. Maybe a few porch lights, a few bowls left out. Quiet. Small. My heart dipped for a moment. But then he added, "If you drive up just one street, you'll find a neighborhood that goes all out. Hundreds of trick-or-treaters. Almost every house is decorated. Lights everywhere." "You'll want to start early to get candy," he grinned. "But if you wait long enough, you'll see it all lit up after dark."

Something loosened inside me. *Hope, tentative but real.* Not right here, but close enough to reach if we were willing. One street away.

We had already started gathering the pieces of what we needed.

The kids' costumes:

A fairy costume for Fay, wings delicate and glittering.
And a grim reaper robe for Landon, complete with a plastic scythe.

I had ordered them weeks earlier, before we even knew exactly where
we would be. Shipped them to the only address we still technically
owned. The skeleton of our flooded house. The house still sagging
against its own swollen frame.

While I picked up the delivered packages, I staked one Halloween
decoration into the ground near the front walkway. A single Styrofoam
gravestone.

It read, "Game Over."

I wedged it between the debris pile, now bigger than the Storage POD
and our car combined, and the entrance to our hollow house.

And I laughed.
A real, sharp cackle.

Not bitter.
Not defeated.
Just... honest.

If nothing else, we still had humor. We still had the stubbornness to
plant a joke in the middle of the ruins.

Across the street, Steve and Lori had their decorations up too. Later
than usual because everything this year was later than usual, but still
there. Lights were strung across the porch. Giant spiderwebs tangled
in the trees. Solar torches flickering against the driveway. The kids had
helped them set it all up. They had stretched cobwebs over everything.

It wasn't perfect, but it looked like Halloween.
It looked like life and death, coexisting.

***

On the weekend before Halloween, Lori surprised the kids with giant gift bags. The bags were stuffed with their favorite candies, snacks and a little toy.

The kind of gift only someone paying close attention knows how to give. A gift that says, I see what you've lost. I see what you're still trying to hold onto. The kids clutched the bags like treasures, beaming.

We were waiting for our flood insurance adjuster to arrive for our inspection, before going to a local trunk or treat. The arrival time window passed and the kids were pacing in their costumes.

I had already done this before, waiting for hours for him to arrive just to find out he wasn't coming. I texted the adjuster and asked if they were still on their way. He replied asking who I was. Like maybe he didn't even know he had us scheduled. *The delayed inspection he had requested.* He told me they were a town over and would be there soon. I asked if we should skip trunk or treating and he told me to leave the door unlocked and he would be there when we returned.

We drove to the trunk or treat event. The kids joined the line and collected candy from each decorated golf cart. One couple was dressed as Hurricane Helene and Milton.

They were pleased with their costumes. I rolled my eyes and told them they owed me a house.

By the time we got back to the house and the kids changed back into their clothes the adjusters pulled up. It was the same duo who had been to our house last year. They remembered us. We talked about last year's restoration and I showed them the pictures.

They did their thing. Going from room to room photographing what was left. Taking pictures and listening to my explanations about what we had removed.

I explained how I was still compiling a list of all of the specific building materials we had used. The adjuster assigned to our case told me that was fantastic, but when we reached our policy limit on the structure's damage, I wouldn't need to be so specific.

This was great news. He seemed pretty confident. We might actually have a chance to pay off our mortgage and get out of here. We just had to wait for the paperwork. It would take longer than last year. *But we could wait a couple months.* We knew it wouldn't be easy, but there was light at the end of the tunnel.

***

On Halloween, the sun was still up when we scarfed down a quick snack, trying to hold ourselves over until trick-or-treating could begin. Greg was finishing his workday, shutting his laptop, just as the kids polished off their last bites and darted off to get changed.

Buckets in hand, they waited by the door. Fay crouched to give Zipper a few extra pets, whispering something only cats and eight-year-olds understand. She adjusted her wings. Landon practiced holding his scythe just right, like a proper grim reaper.

Our first stop was across the street. The neighbors were waiting, smiling, holding out a bowl overflowing with Reese's. Their porch light was already on.

We waved, thanked them, and ran back to our driveway to pile into the car. The real adventure was just beginning. From the backyard, we could already hear the echo of spooky music floating over the trees, as the sun prepared to set. *An invitation from a neighborhood that wasn't ours.*

We parked and stepped into something else entirely.

Every house was lit up, orange lights, glowing skeletons, blow-up dragons and ghosts dancing in the breeze. Families lined the sidewalks. Lawn chairs in driveways. Fire pits flickering in front yards. Bowls of candy, generous and wide.

I wondered if we blended in or if they could tell we were guests. Outsiders, maybe. *Interlopers.*

But then I looked around. There were cars lining both sides of the road. People spilling from vehicles with out-of-state plates. Costumes everywhere. More families than homes. There wasn't any gate keeping here. Not on Halloween.

We weren't the only ones borrowing this street tonight.

House by house, the kids' buckets grew heavier. Our pace slowed from excited skipping to a soft, dragging shuffle. Fay's little legs had worked twice as hard as the rest of ours. By the last stretch, I was carrying her in my arms so she could rest. Greg held the buckets and jackets and masks, all of it slung over his shoulders like he'd done this a hundred times before.

The candy wasn't the only thing full.
Our hearts were too.

We hadn't expected to be this tired. It wasn't even 8 p.m.

But we were starving. And tonight was special, not just Halloween, but our anniversary. Fifteen years since our first date. We decided to celebrate the only way we knew how lately, by finding something that felt like a win.

We pulled into a little sushi restaurant. It was busy, but we found a table. Sat down and peeled off layers of sweat and makeup and tiredness. We ordered too much food and ate like we'd earned it. Because we had.

Halfway through our drive back to the rental, Fay was already asleep. Slumped in her seat, sticky with sugar and dreams. Landon was fighting to stay awake, head leaning against the window, blinking slowly.

I rested my head on Greg's shoulder as he drove.
This is what fifteen Halloweens together looks like.

Borrowed streets. Borrowed joy.
But real, all the same.

22.

Bridge Trolls

After the GoFundMe news article was published, a producer from a London televised docuseries reached out. I was hesitant but also curious.

When I agreed to have a call with the producer, I once again asked "why us?" I reminded them again that there were people elsewhere who probably deserved their attention more than us. They told me they had already done several stories bringing attention to what happened in North Carolina.

This eased my guilt.

Maybe this could be an opportunity. I could provide a different point of view. I could shine a light on what happens to a small forgotten fishing town, when they have experienced repetitive hurricanes. So I talked it over with Greg and the kids.

They agreed. We should do it.

I gave the producer some more information and contacts for additional perspectives. My neighbors, the community center and a local grassroots relief organizer I had connected with.

There was a point where I second-guessed myself and almost backed out of the interview while we were in the planning stages. I reached out to the producer to speak to her off the record. She put my mind at ease and assured me that they would avoid a political angle for our story.

I let out a sigh of relief.

They booked their travel, and we set a date for them to meet with us and film. As the days got closer, I began tracking another storm. I fed them updates in case it became too dangerous for the team to travel here.

Soon before it made landfall, the storm that had the potential to become another destructive hurricane, began to dissipate. So, we continued forward.

When interview day came, we drove back to our house and waited. I could feel my nerves bouncing off each other as we waited for their arrival. I kept myself busy by trying to clean up the house. As if mopping again and sweeping and carrying more debris outside could make it look less damaged and more comfortable for our guests.

I greet them at the door when they arrive. We give them the tour. It's quite short, considering you can see through gaps between the studs. There isn't really a need to do much walking around when it is all in view from the middle of the house.

They prep us for filming, then we sit down to speak to the reporter. The crew and interviewer are incredibly kind. The whole experience runs pretty smoothly. *With the exception of our repetitive nervous tissue crinkling next to our microphone as we speak.*

After taping was finished, we were told editing will take a few weeks. Then they will let us know when it will be airing.

Our interview airs on a news segment right before it's featured in the docuseries. I watch the segment before anyone in the house is awake.

There we were.

Tissues in hand.

My eyes darting around, unable to make eye contact while I speak.

There was a moment in the interview when my composure broke. I started to cry as I recalled when Landon had told me he noticed I don't dance in the kitchen anymore like I used to.

I don't like when anyone sees me cry.
I think that's probably normal.

But here I was crying on television for the whole world to see. I knew the moment it happened, it would be part of the episode. Still, a little part of me hoped it got lost on the cutting room floor during editing.

A few messages roll into my inbox from strangers who wanted to reach out to me after seeing me on their "teles."

Apologies for what we are going through.
Compliments on the way I swing a hammer and push a wheelbarrow.
Thoughts and prayers for our family.

I even befriend one older gentleman who lives alone with no close friends or family. He tells me about what he made for dinner. We chat about the differences between the UK and US. He says he's lonely.

Of course I don't want anyone to be lonely.

Fast forward to after Christmas. I'm overwhelmed and busy packing. I forget to respond to his message. He messages again to tell me I'm a "horrible ignorant woman" for not responding. That was the last time I messaged with him. *Even kindness comes with a price.*

***

Promos, clips, and articles of our interview started popping up on the internet.

When you do these types of things... speaking out publicly, you are told to not go to the comments.

Yet, every single time I do.

I mean, what if someone offered help? *I didn't want to miss it.* So down the rabbit hole of comments I went. Most of them were sympathetic. *Most of them.* But it's hard to remember that, when there are ones that cut deep.

Maybe I am too sensitive.
Maybe I should be able to let these comments roll off me.

But I struggle to do that,
no matter how much I prepare myself.

I can feel my anxiety start to bounce side to side in my hands making my fingers shake as I scroll. My jaw clenches tighter with each cruel word.

It doesn't matter how many times some stranger on a keyboard tells me that I deserve what happened to me, it still makes me recoil. I still wonder why I keep doing this to myself... Thinking that sharing my story or trying to spread information won't keep leaving me vulnerable.

Exposed.

I keep reading though.
I can't stop.

"They are obviously mentally ill for staying"
Did they watch the interview? We desperately want to leave!

"Who cares?"
"It's their own fault!"

"Crying for attention."

"That's what they get for voting for Trump!"
"That's what they get for voting for Biden!"

Oh and then there was one I actually laughed out loud at.
"That's what they get for moving to Florida to avoid wearing a mask during COVID"

Um what? We moved to Florida over a decade ago!

These people don't know me.
They don't want to help.
Even the ones who feel bad.

I thought I was trying to build a bridge.

Let the world see that there are little rural towns like ours that don't make the news. That we had been just as underwater as our neighbors with more recognizable city names.

But I forgot for a moment,
that if you try to build a bridge,
sometimes a troll waits underneath.

23.

Fading Light

There are moments in life when you can feel someone slipping away from you like watching the tide pull back further and further until the shore is nothing but dry, cracked earth.

That's how it felt watching my husband after Hurricane Idalia. His light dimming. His spirit eroding under the weight of something neither of us fully understood at the time.

At first, I told myself it was just stress. Everyone struggles. Everyone has bad days, rough weeks, and difficult seasons. We had just survived an unexpected tragedy, but as the months passed, I realized it was something deeper. There was something clawing at him from the inside out. The man I loved, who once filled our home with laughter and momentum, was becoming a shadow of himself. Still there in body, but his spark was fading.

I tried everything to reach him. I spoke gently when he was distant. I carried the weight of our life when he couldn't bear to lift it. I told myself over and over, *this was just temporary.* We'll get through it. But no matter how much I tried to hold him in place, the truth was undeniable. He was slipping away, and I couldn't stop it.

One evening after our loved ones who helped gut our home had left, we stood in what used to be our dining room. With tears in my eyes, I looked at him and said:

"I've been through a lot in my life, but I know this time I'll get through it because we're in this together. I'm not alone this time."

But little did I know, I was about to feel a familiar feeling. Something from long ago, that I never wanted to experience again.

Something I thought I never would.

True loneliness.

The kind of loneliness that has you standing in a room or going through life surrounded by people, but aching somewhere too deep for language. Loneliness that drives you into the void inside your mind. Where you store away your thoughts and feelings, so no one ever has to see them.

Where the box of burdens stays hidden.

You are walking the line of being too much and not enough. Wishing you could just be what someone needed.

Wishing you could just, be.

After all my years in therapy spent trying to rebuild myself, to reframe, to reshape my life into something sturdy. Taking what was shattered in me and trying to make it whole again. Calling it a mosaic. Trying to believe I was making something beautiful out of something broken *and that meant I wasn't broken anymore.* It didn't seem to matter. Despite all my effort, I was still broken. And now carrying everyone else's anguish so they wouldn't have to feel mine.

I wanted to protect my family from the feeling of dry drowning once the flood waters had receded.

Because while everyone else is celebrating that we made it out alive, we were just trying to hide the fact that we were still choking behind smiles.

I wanted to get through this together, I had said.
I thought I would find peace in knowing I wasn't alone.

But there's nothing peaceful about drowning together.
So I watched my husband jump ship and hoped one day, soon enough, he could return to shore with our children. I wanted to carry the anchors pulling us under.

I had experience with these heavy feelings, the kinds which surface when your life is in upheaval. I was confident I could carry the weight and tread water while they swam.

As a mother, as a wife, you want to shield your family even when you know it won't take all the pain away.

Even when you know, it only makes your pain worth it.

After months of doing what needed to be done and trying to be the pillar in what had become a crumbling Atlantis, I became a shell of myself too. Desperately hoping this empty vessel would stay buoyant.

Then, just as the darkness seemed impenetrable, there was a shift. It wasn't immediate, but it was enough to give me hope. Slowly, he started coming back. His eyes had depth again. His laughter, though rare, was real. I could see him trying. Fighting his way back to us. Back to himself. The flicker of light I had feared was lost forever was still there. For a moment, it felt like maybe this chapter was closing.

But hope is fragile.

Just when his glimmer started to return after Idalia, just when I let myself believe we were finally on the other side of this, life came crashing down again.

Another hurricane.
Another flood.

Another upheaval sent our world spinning.

Helene.

And in the midst of it all, I kept glancing at him. Searching for signs of that dimming light again. I could see the exhaustion in his face, the quiet dread of going through it all again. I wanted to protect him. To somehow try to shield him from it.

But I couldn't.

We were in this together, whether he had the strength for it or not.

I couldn't ignore the look on his face when we stepped into the flooded house for the second time in thirteen months. The thousand-yard stare. Despondency without words. I knew the weight of it could pull him under.

Again I didn't have time to fall apart. I had to act. There were decisions to be made. I had to keep moving. Yet all the while, I kept watching him, searching his face for signs of dimming.

Trying to measure the damage, not just to our home, but to him as well.

Some days, I resented how much I had to hold for all of us last year after Idalia. I wanted to fall apart too, but there was never time or space for it. I wanted someone to catch me. But even in my exhaustion, even in my fury, I loved him too much to let go of hope.

And so, I continued to carry on after Helene. I picked up the broken pieces, willed them to fit. Kept fighting for our family and for our future. I kept hoping. Despite being overcome by the dreadful thought that maybe the moments of calm and tenderness we were maintaining, were just the precursor before the other shoe dropped.

***

As November started, his birthday quickly approached. We were still holding steady after Helene. He continued to stay present when the world kept handing him reasons to fade again.

The kids and I wanted to celebrate him, but he didn't want anything for his birthday. He had said we should spend our money on our daughter's celebration instead because hers was just two days before his. He didn't want a cake or a fancy dinner, just take out. He said this year wasn't worth making a fuss over. *But I couldn't do nothing.*

His dad had passed away when my husband was just seven years old. All he ever had of his father, fit inside a shoebox. A few faded photos, a broken watch, and an old leather wallet, worn bare at the edges. The wallet still had his dad's ID tucked inside. It hadn't been used in decades. An inner flap of leather was coming loose and dangling by a thread.

I made sure to save that shoebox from both floods. We had been carrying it with us to every temporary home to keep it safe.

I snuck into the closet while he was asleep. Retrieved the wallet and put it in my purse. And brought it back to our house with me, so I could work on a gift without anyone knowing. I removed the small rectangle of leather. I cut the broken flap carefully into an hourglass shape. I hand stitched it together folded around a key ring. Smoothed it and sealed the edges. Then hammered in his dad's initials, *which they shared,* on each side.

It wasn't much.
Just leather and thread.

But it was real.
From something carried.
From someone remembered.

From someone my husband wished had been able to be here with him last year.

I made a small box out of thick paper and tape. Tucked the keychain inside. On his birthday, we presented him with the cards we had made and my gift.

To be honest, I was a little embarrassed.
It felt too small.

I'd always tried to make his birthday feel special, not overshadowed by our daughter's. Not forgotten. And now I was handing him a sliver of leather and hoping it meant something.

He opened it slowly.

He didn't say anything at first. He just held it. Turned it over in his hands. Ran his thumb along the edges and surface like he was memorizing the grain. Then he looked at me, *really looked*, and pulled me into a hug so solid and still that it felt like time paused.

"This means more than I know how to say," he whispered.

He didn't attach it to his keys like I had hoped. He carefully attached it to an inside zipper of his computer bag instead. *The one which travels with us even when we aren't fleeing.*

Not because he didn't want to carry it, but because he did. For that reason, carrying it meant protecting it.

And maybe that's what we were doing this time.

Carrying each other.
Protecting what we can.
Stitching something small and steady out of what remains.

Love doesn't always look like grand gestures or fixed houses.

Sometimes it's just remembering the weight they carry quietly. And making sure their story doesn't get lost or overlooked, when they are trying to move forward while carrying it.

24.

Two Worlds

In the months after the hurricane, I started waking up at five A.M. The world was still dark outside the rental windows.

No footsteps yet. No voices yet. Just the hum of the air conditioner. The soft creak of the floor under my steps as I slipped through the house as quietly as I could. Keys in hand, shoes half on, and a bag slung over my shoulder. Trying to close the door with a click I hoped wouldn't wake anyone.

By the time the first edge of sunlight broke through the tree lines, I was already halfway there. Already, heading back to what used to be our home.

But first, my daily stop in to Steve and Lori's for coffee. It had become part of my ritual just as much as building my debris pile.

I let them make me coffee so I can justify staying in the mornings. I don't dare set up my coffee maker at my house because they need this too. It's not just about coffee with neighbors. It's sitting with each other and just being for a moment. It's talking the same thing through for the millionth time without apology. *Since we know one extra detail makes the struggle still relevant.*

We don't try to fix anything. We are in the same boat. We watch the waves crash around us and feel them trying to pull us under. But in these moments, the quiet understanding that can only come from someone holding the same broken paddle as you, means something.

***

I've finished my second cup of coffee and allow myself to admit it's time to head into my house.

The house breathes differently now.
Wet.
Tired.

The volunteers had done so much. They had ripped out the worst of the ruins. Hauled away the pieces too big for me to carry alone, but there was still so much left to do. Piles of half-gutted cabinets. Broken vanities tilting against mold-bloated drywall behind them. Floor tiles cracked into sharp-edged puzzles. Soggy insulation, clinging to the studs like disintegrating cotton candy hiding in places that had been overlooked.

Everywhere I looked, something needed tearing down, carrying out, breaking apart. I worked until my muscles blurred into the work itself.

Cabinets. Sinks. Wall tile. Rust covered tools abandoned in the garage. I mop floors, I knew would never feel clean again no matter how many passes of bleach they had gotten. I vacuum sludge and drywall dust until the shop vac coughed and whined. And begged for a break, I didn't have time to give it.

I continue to document everything for insurance just in case. My fingers grimy on the phone screen, the photos blurring as sweat dripped into my eyes.

The work isn't efficient. It isn't always the most strategic. It is just survival, one ruined piece at a time.

By midday, the weight in my limbs felt different. Not just tiredness.

A heavy liquid ache seeping into my bones when they stop asking for permission to collapse. It's the slow betrayal of a body that had already learned once, long before this flood or the first one, how to keep moving long after it should have stopped.

I knew this feeling. I had worn it before.

The blurred edges.
The trembling hands.
The drag of legs that carried grief as much as weight.

Running on fumes wasn't new. It was a second skin. A second skin I thought I had shed too many times to count over the years.

***

By noon, I drove back across town. The rental felt like a different country. Inside, there was furniture to sit on, a place to rest. The floor was solid under my feet. I showered the dust off my skin, changed into clean clothes and stepped into the second half of my day.

Homeschool projects with the kids while my husband toiled away at his laptop. Dinner at the table with laughter tucked carefully between forkfuls. Board games. Movies. Snippets of normal life stitched together like a patchwork quilt we refused to let unravel.

It was like living two full days for every one written on the calendar. I was traveling between two worlds.

One world built from walls that still stood.
One built from walls stripped down to their ribs.

One where survival meant paperwork and schedules.
One where survival meant muscle memory and stubbornness.

After hours of working alone at the house, I carried dust in the creases of my elbows. Even after the water would run clear in the shower I never felt quite clean.

I filled my days with lists and plans. I hammered the next tasks into the cracks before the resentment over the repetition could seep through. Some days, the silence caught me off guard detouring my scheduled activities.

Grief rose up fast. It choked me. It seeped out through my eyes when I bent to lift a fallen door, or ran my hand across the scarred concrete slab that used to be where our kitchen cabinets stood.

If I broke down,
this was where I did it.

Hidden inside the emptied rooms, where no one could see me tear open and mend myself closed again in the same breath.

Physical exhaustion.
Mental exhaustion.
Emotional exhaustion.

These weren't strangers. They were companions I had learned to walk alongside long before the floods came. Maybe it started with the older storms, the ones no one else could see. Maybe it started with learning too young, how to rebuild yourself in secret. Maybe it sharpened after the first flood, when I realized there was no cavalry coming once the emergency of it all faded. Just me left with my own two hands.

Either way, I didn't need to learn how to endure.
I already knew.

And so I did what I had always done. I flipped the switch. Pressed it all down where it wouldn't be seen. Walked back into the rental house with a smile tucked carefully into place. I held the pieces together. Held the line for my kids, my husband, and myself.

Fake it until you make it.

I didn't just tell them it was going to be okay. I let myself believe it. On the grounds that sometimes the only thing more dangerous than a lie is the truth which leaves you frozen in place. Hope isn't something you carry easily when you've learned how easily it shatters.

You carry it the way you carry a cracked plate, gingerly, carefully, without setting it down until you absolutely have to. And still, I carried it. Because persistence is showing up anyway.

I was living in both worlds at once.

The broken and the borrowed.
Until I couldn't tell the difference anymore.

25.
Still Standing in Grief

I've never been good at keeping friends.

I clung to the excuses of circumstance. People move, they get busy, and sometimes they just drift. Though, even before the floods, I knew I was always bending myself into something easier to hold. Not too intense, not too quiet, not too complicated or too blunt. I didn't always read the room right. I missed cues I didn't know were there. Sometimes I didn't even know people were playing a game, until I lost.

Yet when people left, they insisted it wasn't about me.
It didn't make it hurt less.

After Idalia, more disappeared. Some stopped checking in and some never started. I told myself it was understandable. *It was expected.* Even reasonable. I reminded myself, we couldn't be everyone's emergency forever.

So when Helene hit, there weren't many people left to lose. Yet still, somehow, I did.

When the walls of my house literally fell away again, I remembered how fast the calls can stop. *How quickly people can look away.*

It wasn't usually a big betrayal.
More often just a quiet retreat.

I didn't lose them in the floods. I lost them in the silence that came after. There weren't fights. No screaming. No accusations. Just... nothing. Absence that doesn't echo, it absorbs.

When the water came for our house again, I had sent out updates. My friends and loved ones responded at first. Asked how we were. Said they couldn't imagine what we were going through.

Some people even donated to the fundraiser. *I'll always be thankful. It helped in real, tangible ways.* But money doesn't replace emotional presence. It doesn't check if you're still breathing steadily. It doesn't pull you off the floor when your knees buckle. It doesn't watch you scrub mold from the wall where your daughter's paintings used to hang.

I don't think anyone meant harm. *I really don't.* But it doesn't make the silence sting less.

As days stretched to weeks and weeks to months, most of them disappeared. Like I'd become a chapter they weren't interested in rereading. As if I no longer fit into the rhythm of their lives because of what I was experiencing.

I tried to be realistic. I tried to not ask for anything big. Not solutions or daily check-ins.

Just someone to stay present.

They were the people I would've checked on if roles were reversed. I wouldn't have hesitated. *Not because I'm better. But because that's who I thought we were to each other.*

But the silence grew until it swallowed what we used to be to each other. And when people faded out of view, I rehearsed their apology for them.

I softened their absence with reasons they never gave.

Maybe their lives were heavy too. Maybe they didn't know what to say. *Maybe they were afraid of what I might say.* Maybe pretending I was okay made it easier for them to keep their distance. Maybe they thought I didn't need them.

Maybe I didn't.

Even so, it's not the same thing as being okay. That kind of strength doesn't feel noble. *It just feels lonely.*

And I grieved them all quietly, in layers. While holding a trash bag full of waterlogged memories. While reapplying for disaster aid. While explaining to my kids why we couldn't go back home.

It's not that we needed saving. We just needed to be truly seen without looking away when it got uncomfortable. Bereavement after disaster doesn't just take your home, it takes your illusion of who stays.

Some people are built for urgency, but not for aftermath. They don't have the stamina for rot. Or for silence. Or for the fifteenth retelling of the same story, now with less hope in your voice.

I was too raw to be a lesson yet.
So they left.

Maybe some will come back.
Maybe not.
But I've stopped writing their apologies for them.

You can be grateful for what you received and still grieve what went missing. Both are true. Both have always been true. I live in that contradiction now. *I don't try to frantically fix it anymore.*

Survival isn't a montage or a climax. It's sorting through ruined precious things and deciding what's worth carrying forward. It's learning that care sometimes has an expiration date *and trying to convince yourself you're okay with that.*

Standing in the ruins of your life, holding both the gratitude and the abandonment.

Not choosing one or trying to untangle them.
Just balancing both. Without dropping either.

Some days, the gratitude wins.
Some days, the grief.

Most days, they sit in my hands together.

Heavy.
Uneven.
Permanent.

26.

The Middle Gear

There's a kind of quiet that sets in after the initial shock wears off. Not peace, not clarity, just a slow dulling of urgency, as the adrenaline drains and the paperwork continues. That's where we were.

Between seasons.
Between housing.
Between holidays.
Between decisions.

Stuck in the part where hope hadn't died, but it was starting to limp. We were waiting for answers. Not the kind you ask friends or neighbors for. The kind you only get from systems. From departments and agencies. And workflows so massive and overflowing, you wonder if your name can even fit inside them.

There was no precedent for Greg. A remote worker, still operational, and still performing.

But stuck in a disaster zone.

He wasn't supposed to exist.
Not like this.

It's strange being a cog that's both acknowledged and somewhat invisible. Like being told you're essential and also somehow in the way. We were told not to lose hope. They were still watching. Still advocating, behind the scenes. *And yet the silence between updates grew louder each week.*

We began to make decisions slowly, measured in modular chunks. Nothing too permanent. Nothing we couldn't undo.

On the grounds that, what if the miracle came through?

What if his relocation finally happened? What if everything we'd waited for, and were told should work out, was suddenly available and we had accidentally planted roots too deep to leave? We lived like settlers squatting on rented land. Temporary by design, hopeful by necessity, paralyzed by logistics.

I started to feel like the only thing we were actually doing was waiting.

Waiting for our requests to make it to the right people.
Waiting for a relocation path to unlock.
Waiting for a slot to open.
Waiting to be remembered again.

And while we waited, we adjusted. We survived in place and my husband kept showing up. He kept delivering. Kept proving despite the chaos, he could still function.

And that, somehow, became the problem.

It started to feel like the very thing we thought would help us, was now the reason we weren't getting helped. He hadn't cracked yet. He was still dependable. Still efficient. He was still keeping the engine running without complaint. Even if the pistons were grinding and the oil was long gone.

Why fix something still operating?
Why prioritize what hasn't failed yet?
We didn't want to fail just to be seen. *Although sometimes, it felt like*

the only remaining lever to pull.

Still, he kept going.
Still, we waited.

He was a squeaky gear in a machine that needed him to keep spinning. Not so loud he caused alarm, not so slow he caused delay. Just loud enough to be noticed, yet small enough to delay fixing.

Every so often, there'd be a pulse of new information.

A rumor.
A maybe.

A sense, someone behind the curtain was still moving pieces. And then... nothing. Doors would close. Timelines for assistance slid. Requests floating from one person's desk to another.

We recalculated.
Rebudgeted.
Recalibrated what it meant to hold out hope.

We weren't giving up. But we weren't sure what we were holding out for anymore, either. There was no map for this. Only a sense of duty. Maybe a little stubbornness. Of choosing not to slam the door on something, even if it never quite opened for us. So we stayed in motion. Small motions. Strategic motions.

He stayed the middle gear. Waiting for the moment someone would realize the machine was running dry. And hoping, quietly, wearily, it would happen before we broke down.

27.

Disdain for Resilience

I've grown to hate the word resilient.
It's often meant as a compliment.
But it always feels like a diagnosis.

"You must be resilient."
"You'll bounce back."
"You've got this."

What it really means is:

You'll survive even if no one helps you.
You can be ignored
because you always land on your feet.

Even when your legs are broken.
Even when the ground is gone.

I know people mean well.
But resilient is just the language people use
to exit the conversation.

Spare me the echoes of borrowed wisdom.
The hollow stitched-together phrases.
Draped over wounds like thin white gauze.
As if covering pain could make it vanish.

I want to be soft.
To rest in the ruin.
Not mend what I never shattered.

I breathe the air thick with platitudes.
Polluted with expectations,
I never agreed to meet.

Let me be broken.
un-mended, unpolished, undone.

I am tired of stitching strength,
from seams meant to give way.
I want to take a seam ripper
to your threads of obligation.

Your woven demands.
Your entitled gaze.

"You're so strong" they say.
As if I wouldn't trade it all,
for the chance to be held instead.

"She's supposed to be resilient."

You let them gnaw at my roots.
Then gasped when I wilted.

"Show us how you overcome!" they say.

You don't want me,
only the performance of resilience.

Speak if you must.
But make it real.
Or let the quiet do what it does best.

28.

Pick-Me-Up

Last year, we originally thought the county would come to help.

That's what they said, just put everything at the curb, we'll take care of it. I remember sorting the piles like it mattered. Like the distinction meant anything to anyone but me. It all rotted anyway. And when nothing got picked up, we paid for every single load ourselves. Five large dumpsters. For thousands of pounds of everything we had lost.

This year, we didn't wait. We rented a dumpster the moment we could and filled it with as much of our soaked belongings as we could.

We knew the drill.

We continued to gut the house and stacked the remaining debris high in the front yard. It was substantially larger than the storage pod. I kept staring at it and thinking, this pile is what's left of structure. Of effort. Of all the time we spent trying to make it livable again. And now it's trash. Again.

I wasn't going to be skipped. Not this time.

I started emailing the county right away. I didn't care if I sounded desperate. I was. I begged them not to forget about our street. Every few days, a neighbor would stop me and ask, "Any updates?" "Are they coming?" I told them confidently "I'm on it. I won't let it happen again."

151

But honestly, I wasn't sure if I believed myself.

I made more calls. Sent more emails. Wrote out two signs fashioned from left over building materials and paint. One for the main road. One to be placed halfway down the street. *Just in case.* I kept thinking, maybe if I make us more visible, louder, more annoying, maybe then we'll count.

Debris trucks moved through surrounding neighborhoods. I tracked them. Refused to give up until I knew for sure. Then one day the blinking road sign downtown changed: "Pickup complete." I read it three times and felt my stomach drop. *I really thought that was it.* I thought I had failed again.

Then, days later, they finally arrived.

***

It was now December. Almost three months after Helene.

I sent out the text. "They're here!" We all rushed to the curb with the last of what we hadn't dared to put out yet. I made sure every pile was sorted exactly the way they instructed. I didn't want them to have any excuse to skip us. Not now. *Not after all that.*

Lori and I stood in her driveway and watched them. She handed out water. We stood in the shade of the garage and watched the bobcat and the bucket truck scoop up the damage. They were huge, these machines. One of them taller than our houses. Yet they moved in almost a nimble way. Fluid even. Like it was an interpretive mechanically performed dance.

One lifted, the other caught.

It was strange how graceful destruction could look when done with precision.

We clapped. We cheered. I took a video to send to Greg. He was working, but he needed to see it. We needed a win, *even if it was just a clean lawn.*

The relief hit harder than I expected. Not because the work was done *because it definitely wasn't.* But because it no longer looked like the indoors had overflowed and spilt out to the outdoors. The inside was still gutted. But outside, it looked like a yard again. Like the world might start over if we just kept showing up for it.

Lori and I hugged. Then we got to work.

We raked what was left behind into bins. I pulled out my magnetic nail roller and started scanning our yards, listening for the tiny clicks of rusted metal. I couldn't stop. I kept going down the whole road. Driveway to driveway. House by house. It felt a little obsessive, but last year I had gotten three flat tires in a month. Nails we couldn't even see. I didn't want that again.

Not for us.
Not for Lori.
Not for anyone on our street.

Some things shouldn't have to be endured twice. *If I couldn't keep the water out, I could at least keep the nails out of everyone's tires.*

29.
Snow Globe Ambitions

We had packed away Christmas alongside the individually wrapped ornaments, the ribbon, the string lights, and the carefully coiled garland. Everything tucked into plastic bins and totes, sealed and stacked neatly inside the Storage POD. We weren't supposed to need them in Florida this year. We were supposed to be somewhere new, filled with wonder, relief, and holiday cheer.

That dream broke open with the tides from the hurricane.

When floodwaters surged through the cracks of the container. They didn't just soak our belongings, they disintegrated our children's handmade ornaments. They shattered the heirloom porcelain Christmas village.

What was left of our decorations amounted to one-third of an artificial Christmas tree. The middle section. *We'd forgotten it in the attic.* Dry. Intact. But how do you decorate with just the torso of a tree?

No base.
No top.
No way to stand it upright.

I know the holidays aren't supposed to be about trees or garland or presents. In spite of knowing that, something still felt off this year. We had made it through Thanksgiving full of gratitude for each other, for still being present with each other. But when it came to Christmas, the spark was gone.

There would be no gifts. We had no space for toys, no room for extra things. We couldn't justify buying a new tree, knowing it might be tossed onto the next debris pile. The idea of decorating a salt-damaged bush outside a home we didn't live in, felt more sad than symbolic.

We had tried the year before. Tried to do the full thing. The joy, the decorations, the unwrapping, the assembling of toys. But joy had been gutted alongside our rooms this time.

Pretending again would feel like complicity. *Like a chosen delusion.*

But still. We needed something.

I needed to see our children light up again like Christmas candles. Even if only for a moment.

We needed something honest.
Something humble.
Something different.

Our rental ended on December sixteenth. We didn't know where we'd go next. Holiday pricing had kicked in. We were being priced out of our own county, competing with vacationers in our search for shelter.

So, we decided to leave.
Just for a little while.

*　*　*

We found a rental in Western Massachusetts, less than an hour from my sister. A sublet from a timeshare resort I had stayed at as a kid. The price was half of what we were paying in Florida. It felt like fate. The kids squealed. They might see snow for the first time.

We booked it immediately.

Then the reservation was canceled by the hosting site. Then rebooked. Then canceled again. It wasn't a glitch. The condo wasn't ready for guests. The manager apologized. They couldn't honor the stay.

Still, I didn't want to give up the idea. I didn't want to give up the dream. But rentals were now completely out of reach, especially when we factored in travel expenses. So, I stopped looking for a house. I started looking for shelter.

A hotel.

I called Best Western. I booked over the phone, something which I rarely do. *I just needed to talk to a person.* She listened. She asked questions. She found every possible discount. It felt like she wanted this trip for us as much as we did. Not just to meet a quota, but because she had listened to our story and recognized what I was trying to do. *What I was trying to save.*

We had a plan. A confirmed reservation. A place which couldn't be canceled or repriced or quietly disappear.

That's the thing about hotels, you may give up a kitchen, a dining room, a backyard, but you gain accountability.

I'd trade square footage for something that couldn't be taken away. It didn't matter if their kindness was maybe just corporate policy. It was reliable. And reliability is what we craved.

The hotel wasn't downtown. It wasn't a resort. It wasn't within walking distance of the lights or events. It was a stand-alone building on the edge of Pittsfield Massachusetts, mostly used for business travel.

And that's what we were now. Not vacationers. Not locals. Just a displaced family in the business of survival.

Looking for dependability.
Far from the waterline.

***

We packed every item of winter clothing we could cobble together. Most of our trips north were during warm seasons. But we had enough to layer. We bought winter coats. Not just outerwear but investments. Symbols of a future we still hoped for.

A future with hills instead of flood zones. Blizzards instead of hurricane warnings. Where fish didn't swim through the living room. Where shelter meant protection, not just more disaster to escape.

The trip was on. I texted my mother-in-law and called my sister. They were giddy. They hadn't seen us since before Helene.

We dropped off our summer clothes. Loaded the coats. And said goodbye to our cat, Zipper.

Steve asked the kids to bring back a snowball. They agreed.

Then we hit the road.

We knew the drive before we took it. Eighteen hours on paper. Closer to twenty-four in practice. We knew the rhythm of it. The initial excitement. The mid-drive slump. The second wind and how it hits when you're past the halfway point, but still so far from done.

We knew the rest-stops with the sticky floors and the machines that always eat your quarters. We knew the gas stations that smell like burnt coffee and ammonia. But most importantly we had committed to memory the ones with the cleanest bathrooms.

We had memorized the turnpike tolls that remind you how many states you've crossed and the predictable traffic jam areas. We could anticipate the moment where the temperature changes and your body forgets the Florida heat and humidity for long enough to feel like maybe you've earned a shiver.

We weren't heading into the unknown.

We were returning to something familiar. Our family's version of snowbird migration. Not for pleasure, not exactly, but for something that had always felt like a pause.

Like rebalancing.
Like escape.

We'd done this drive for years. Usually in the summer, timed around school breaks and the cheapest gas prices. Always tight on budget, but wide on wonder.

The car was full and the kids had their usual snacks and their games and their playlists, but they also had new questions this time:

How much snow would there be?
Do you think we could go sledding?
Do you think we could build a real snowman?

They didn't ask where we were going to live after. Maybe they knew better. *Maybe they were waiting to follow our lead.*

We stopped less this time. There's something about fleeing, even gently, that keeps you from lingering. We just wanted to get there. To arrive somewhere that hadn't already fallen apart.

We watched the sun cross over North Carolina. Watched it burn orange behind bare trees in Virginia. Watched the light shift again and again as we moved north, leaving behind palm trees, flooded roads, a house we no longer trusted and a coastline that felt like it had turned against us.

Somewhere in New York, it started to snow. Just light flakes. Wisps really. But it was enough to make the kids press their faces to the windows. It was enough to make the road feel different. Like we were being invited forward.

We were close. Just a couple hours to go. We pulled into a small gas station in a tiny town none of us had ever heard of. The kind of place that doesn't show up in memory until it's attached to something that matters to you.

The kids asked if they could get out. Just for a minute.

They wanted to see the snow up close while Greg refueled the car. I hesitated. "It's cold," I warned. "Really cold." They weren't dressed for it. Not fully. Layered, yes. But no gloves. Hoodie zippers half-up. Hats slightly askew.

It didn't matter. No amount of discouraging could convince them that waiting until we got to the hotel would feel just as good. So they jumped out, puffing into the air like it was a magic trick. We walked to the side of the building, where a narrow patch of greenery had caught a soft drift of snow.

They approached it slowly, reverently, like they were studying each individual flake before it melted.

"Can we touch it?" they asked in unison, eyes wide.
I sighed. "I don't know… it might be dirty. And your hands are going to freeze without gloves."

They didn't care.
"Please!" they begged again.

I gave in. "Okay. But please don't touch any dirty snow. And absolutely avoid anything yellow!" I laughed. They nodded seriously. Stepped carefully toward a low bush coated in powder. Scooped the snow into their bare hands like it was treasure.

Their eyes lit up.
Awe.
Validation.

As if they'd just confirmed it was real.

"Please don't eat it," I added. They rolled their eyes at the accusation.

"I wasn't gonna," Fay grinned.
"It feels like holding a slushie with no cup," Landon declared, cheeks pink from the cold.

Greg watched us from across the parking lot, gas pump in hand. He tilted his head toward me and I tilted mine back. He joined us a minute later, pulled the kids into a hug. We stood there for one slow minute together, letting the snow flurry around us. Letting it land on our shoulders and stick to our sleeves.

Then we got back in the car. Heat blasting and windows fogged. Back on the road. Still inching toward rest.

We weren't going to our next home.
We weren't going to solve anything,

But for a few days, in a town tucked inside a snow globe, we were going to rest.

30.

Best Western in the North East

We pulled up to the overhang at the hotel entrance and stepped out of the car. I shivered from the frigid air and maybe a little from the excitement of finally arriving.

Greg started unpacking. Suitcase by suitcase, the windows became unblocked by the puzzle of our belongings. I went inside to check us in. I knew what it looked like. We'd arrived with more than the average guests.

"Oh, so you'll be staying with us for a while," the man at the front desk said.

"Yeah. We're from Florida. Displaced from the hurricanes," I answered. "We couldn't find housing during the holidays, so we figured... might as well make the best of it. We're visiting family."

His face shifted, cordial, then grim, then back to cordial. "I'm so sorry to hear that. Please let me know if there's anything we can do. If you need anything, just ask."

I held myself back from saying, "Well, if you mean anything... Do you know someone who wants to buy my house?"

Wrong place, wrong time.

We took the elevator to the second floor. It took several trips to bring everything to our suite, hauling luggage, laundry baskets and plastic bags. There was so much more space than we expected. It was exactly what we needed. *It had enough breathing room to settle in for two weeks.*

Every morning, we went down for breakfast. It became one of our favorite parts of the day.

It seemed like everyone here knew us now. Each person who worked the front desk or walked the halls or could be found in gathering areas, I had conversed with them all. They had become invested in our family.

As if the hotel had become our personal temporary neighborhood.

The Director of Operations, Anthony, one day surprised us with a small pine tree in a pot so the kids could have a Christmas tree. He gave them holiday crafts and let us display the painted nutcrackers in the lobby. Anthony even scraped ice off our windshield because we didn't own an ice scraper.

And each time we returned from a day out, the staff greeted us with "Welcome home!"

And it did, in an unexpected way,
kind of feel like home.

***

A few days in, it snowed. The kids asked to play outside. We suited up in cold-weather gear. "Living in Florida had thinned our blood," I joked to Greg.

We had a snowball fight in the courtyard. The kids made snow angels in the parking lot. Together, we built a tiny snowman with gravel for eyes and propped him on a table near the back entrance.

The next day, the snow kept falling.

I looked out the window to check how much had accumulated and saw Anthony quietly fixing the snowman we had built. *He didn't know we saw him. But we did.*

My sister texted to say the hill behind her house was ready for sledding. Sledding! The kids had only seen it in movies. We started getting ready.

But first, we tidied up our temporary home.

Trash accumulates quickly in a hotel room. We hadn't requested turndown service. It felt weird to have someone clean up after us while we were living there. Instead, we exchanged towels when the staff prepped other rooms. We filled a couple grocery bags with garbage and stealthily snuck them into the large bins in the breakfast lounge.

This time one of the workers caught us mid-act and offered us real trash bags. Fay giggled all the way back to our room.

It was time to load into the car and drive toward the mountains. My sister and brother-in-law's property backs up to the Adirondack trails.

When we arrived, we ran toward the house, trying not to slip on the ice. The warm air hugged us the second we stepped inside. So did they. We greeted each other with giant hugs. Not much time had passed and the kids could barely contain themselves any longer. They were squirming while we adults tried to finish our conversations.

My sister and her husband noticed.
"Okay, are you ready?"
"Yes!" Landon and Fay shouted.

We layered up and headed outside.

My sister said the snow might be too fluffy for sledding.
"Aunty Tiffy, it's perfect!" Fay declared.

Climbing uphill through the snow was harder than I remembered. But the kids didn't care. They tripped and crawled their way up, determined. At the top, we showed them how to sit and hold on. I could tell Landon was a little nervous because he's not a fan of heights.

But he wanted this moment and nothing was going to stop him.

I always tell the kids "You can't be brave unless you're scared. If you're not scared, you're just doing something."

They must have been listening. Landon decided to be brave and volunteered to go first.

Snow pelted his face.
Eyes squeezed shut.
Fingers white-knuckled on the orange sled.

When he reached the bottom, he was beaming. "That was awesome!" he yelled. *His eyes looked like they'd forgotten the whole last year.*

It was Fay's turn. She climbed into an inflatable tube. "Push me, Uncle Sam!" She sped down the hill, gliding over the snow, barely sinking. Greg had to dive to stop her from hitting the fence. She loved it!

We all took turns, over and over again. Even my sister's dog, Apollo, wanted in. I let him pull me on the sled. He got so excited he flung me into the snow halfway down and ran off with my ride.

We kept going until we couldn't climb anymore. The kids' cheeks were rosy. Their noses dripped. Their hands were frozen from taking off their gloves.

This was exactly what we had hoped for.

***

The very next day, my mother-in-law arrived at our hotel.

She drove over two hours by herself to see us. When she arrived, arms full of Christmas gifts, she hugged each of us so tightly I thought she might not let go. And I think I would've been okay with that. We missed her as much as she missed us.

Greg introduced her to the hotel staff.
"This is my mom," he told them.
"Welcome, Mom!" they replied.

We showed off the hats we'd been knitting. Updated her on the strange details of our Florida life. Told her about the house, the insurance waiting game, and the rentals. It felt good to say it out loud to someone who already knew the backdrop.

We went out for lunch, just the five of us. The restaurant was warm and cozy, strung with white lights and soft music. Eating with another tourist made us feel like vacationers instead of transients. Like maybe we were meant to be there.

Back at the hotel, the kids opened their gifts. They immediately began trying everything out, trying things on, spreading joy across every surface of the room. We all played a new game involving spoons, hunched around the coffee table, elbows bumping, rules bending. We did Mad Libs until we cried from laughter. Then we curled up and watched a movie together before bed.

My mother-in-law insisted on sleeping on the couch.
She wouldn't let either kid give up their bed.
Not even for one night.

"They've been displaced enough," she said.
And she was right, they had.

The next morning, we introduced her to our hotel breakfast. The waffle machine, the eggs and bacon in the warmer, the staff who greeted her like she belonged. Then it was time for her to leave. She had a long drive ahead, and people were coming to her house for Christmas Day.

She wished she could stay longer.
So did we.

But we were grateful.

Grateful she came to visit, even if it was shorter than we wanted. I found myself wishing we could pack her up and bring her back with us to Florida. Maybe she wished we could stay with her instead.

Stay somewhere safe.
Somewhere away from hurricanes.

31.

Not Ours to Keep

We tried to make our hotel room feel like Christmas.

The desk in the living room area became a makeshift holiday corner. The small tree the hotel gave us sat next to decorations from my mother-in-law. We made paper garlands and taped them to the wall. *It wasn't extravagant, but it was ours.* A taped together reminder that holidays could still exist inside the anguish of a year.

My sister invited us for a Christmas Eve sleepover. The kids were excited at first. But the day before, Fay grew quiet. "Do you think Auntie Tiffy would be upset if I didn't want to sleep over?" she asked. "I still want to celebrate, I just don't want to sleep in another bed."

I pulled her close. "Auntie would be proud of you for saying how you feel," I said.

Fay explained that she was just getting used to the hotel. More change felt like too much. We all understood. We decided to shift the festivities to a few hours earlier. Then we could head back to the hotel before bedtime. We celebrated our new plan with the unlimited hot chocolate in the lobby with extra marshmallows.

The next morning, we had our usual breakfast and greeted our hotel family. Then we packed the car and headed to Tiffany and Sam's. The roads twisted through snow-covered hills. It felt like we were driving through a holiday movie.

169

When we arrived the dogs greeted us first, tails wagging. Inside, the air smelled like garlic, pine, and something waiting to be enjoyed for dessert. Tiffany and Sam were finishing dinner. The kids pointed out the porcelain Christmas village. They moved across the room to search the tree for ornaments they'd made years ago.

Tiffany offered to give them back, knowing how much we had lost. But Landon, in his matter-of-fact voice, said, "No, those are yours now. They don't belong on our next tree. We'll visit them next year."

We decorated stockings with puffy paint and placed them by a fan to dry. We turned a table for two into one which could seat six. Tiffany had asked what would feel like home on a plate, so Fay piled her plate high with buttered noodles. Not the microwave packet kind, but real ones, boiled on a stove.

After dinner, the stockings were still drying so Sam and Tiffany handed out shopping bags full of stocking stuffers. Souvenirs from work trips. Landon's favorite candy. Scented colored pencils for Fay. A spice challenge gummy worm. Road trip games and fidget toys. *The kind of thoughtful, chosen gifts that feel like love designed just for us.*

Christmas delivered in grocery bags.

That night at the hotel, the kids fell asleep without protest. Greg and I sat up for a while, not wrapping presents, just existing. "Today was a good day!" he said. "I'm glad we did that."

The next morning was slow. Calm. The kids video-chatted with Greg's sister and opened the gifts she'd sent. We skipped a big lunch, keeping it light. Instead, we chose to stuff our pockets and my purse with candy before heading to the theater downtown.

The theater had heated recliners. We peeled off our coats, scarves, hats, and gloves. It was quiet. Comfortable.

When we got back to the hotel Landon climbed into his bed. He said he wanted cucumbers. "I can't just eat junk-food!" he declared. We cut up his extra snack, then he went to bed early.

Something in him had already shut down. A couple hours later, his skin felt warm. He had a fever. *Sometimes he doesn't even notice when he's getting sick. He just pushes through until his body stops giving him a choice.*

In the morning while Landon was still sleeping, I got dressed to go buy medicine. That's when I realized it, my engagement ring was gone. I assumed I'd taken it off before my shower, but it wasn't on the counter or the nightstand. We turned the whole hotel room upside down searching.

I remembered seeing it on my hand on the car ride over to the movie theater. I must have lost it when taking off my gloves.

Cold weather shrinks your fingers.
I had forgotten.

Greg went back to search. The parking lot, the theater floor, between and under the seat cushions with the assistance of the staff. Nothing.

I posted in a local group I found online.

A white gold diamond ring, lost on Christmas Day at the Phoenix Theatres Beacon Cinema. We couldn't afford to offer a reward. We were only visiting, after losing our home in Florida.

The post spread quickly. Strangers shared it, messaged me, and offered help. One woman lent me her metal detector. I dug through snow until my hands went numb. People recognized me from the post. Some even stopped to help search.

We called the theater again, pawn shops and the police station. Asking them if it was turned in. Still, nothing.

Just when things started to feel a little okay again.
When the kids smiled,
and the noodles were real,
something else was lost.

It felt like the river had one more thing to steal.
The ring didn't turn up.

Sometimes what matters most isn't what's recovered. It's that, when
something is lost, someone shows up to help you look. *That's at least
what I tried to tell myself.*

We didn't want to leave. Not just because it meant giving up on my
ring. Or because it meant returning to Florida, to the flood-torn shell
of our town. But because for a few weeks, we had touched something
like stability.

Something like peace.
We didn't want to let it go.

We visited Tiffany and Sam one more time to say goodbye. We
dropped off things we wouldn't need back in Florida, snow pants,
gloves, layers of warmth we wouldn't be needing again for a long time.
They promised to hold onto them for us, and we promised to come
back. We regifted the little pine tree so they could plant it on their
property. Hoping soon enough, we would be able to watch it grow
here.

We said goodbye to the hotel staff. The ones who welcomed us like
they meant it.

We were heading home to see our cat and repack our suitcases for a
wedding. To see friends, to put on real clothes, to smile for pictures.

***

Upon our return to Florida, we thanked Steve and Lori for taking good care of Zipper. Fay made sure Steve knew she hadn't forgotten his snowball. We giggled as we handed him a Ziploc bag we had filled with water.

"Sorry it melted," she said.

He laughed, holding it like a fragile treasure and for just a moment, it felt like we had carried a bit of winter home.

32.

No Fixed Address

We live out of suitcases, trash bags and laundry bins now.

Neatly packed at first. Clothes folded into careful piles with belongings zipped into pouches. But the care wears off with every move. By the fourth or fifth time, it's just survival: shove what fits, throw the rest in the trunk, figure it out later.

Later never comes.

The first few rentals felt like decent compromises. Then, somehow, as time passed the rentals got continually worse.

More expensive.
Less stocked.
Less safe.

One had a washer which broke slowly over the two weeks we stayed. It wasn't balanced, no matter how light the load or how carefully we arranged the clothing. It bucked like a bull halfway through every spin cycle, dragging itself forward until it slammed into the wall.

We told the owner. "Oh yeah, sometimes I have to put my whole weight on it until it calms down!" she laughed and said she should probably replace it soon. We tried to lean on it. Braced it. But somehow the machine kept fighting us during every use.

I stood there one afternoon wondering if this was it. If we were going to flood someone else's house with a load of damp socks and wind up re-salvaging all our things again. Eventually, it broke for good. The owner apologized and replaced it quickly. But the feeling stayed.

Even when we were paying to stay dry, we weren't safe from more water damage.

Kitchens gave the illusion of function, rows of matching plates, a stack of clean pans, a little tray with salt and pepper. Until you go to load your groceries and you realize half the fridge shelves are missing. Or until you started cooking and realized there was no colander, pan lids, baking sheets or actual salt in the salt shaker.

I once had to dig through our car's glove compartment for fast food salt packets so we could finish making dinner. Another time, I found myself washing vegetables in a plastic cereal bowl because there was no clean strainer.

I started grocery shopping with an eye toward what was missing in the houses instead of what we needed to eat.

One night, I bought a kitchen-sized trash can along with my groceries. At self-checkout, I loaded everything directly into the bin to avoid plastic bags. A stranger called it "ingenuity." I called it necessary. The rental at the time had a bathroom-sized can in the kitchen. Totally fine if you're there for three days, eating mostly at restaurants. Totally not fine, if you're cooking all your own meals for four weeks.

Some places had bugs.
Some had mystery odors.
Some had handles to cabinets barely clinging on with glue instead of bolts.

One had a bathroom sink that barely drained and when Greg investigated, he pulled out a plastic hair clip from a previous tenant.

Another had screaming, gunshots and sirens echoing from nearby.

We started inspecting every place like amateur home inspectors. Not for charm or location, but for signs of post-hurricane rot.

Loose grout.
Peeling caulk.
The telltale warping of once-wet drywall behind the curtains.

Each time we moved, we asked ourselves: "Is this ours or the rental's?" A vegetable peeler, a pillow, extra towels.

Some items we had bought after the first flood.
Some items were purchased after the second.
Some had survived both.

We were borrowing from ourselves to equip a place we were paying to live in. *Now, we couldn't tell the difference.*

We joked about starting a consulting service for short-term rentals. We'd stay a few days, make a report, and tell the owners what they were missing. We'd suggest where to hang towel hooks, which utensil drawer was missing a can opener, whether the condition of their grout was about to cause structural damage. *Maybe then we'd get a few free nights out of it.*

By the end of the first week of January, we had stayed in 6 different houses that weren't ours, with 3 hotels sprinkled in between. A total of nine places in four months that we had tried to call home, without ever really believing it. I stopped fully unpacking after the third move. Everything we owned stayed half-buried in garbage bags and suitcases.

No fixed address.
No fixed anything.

33.

The Noise That Knew Me

I don't think I've ever fully explained what this has cost me. Not just in housing or stability, but neurologically. Internally.

Burnout is real for anyone, but when you're autistic, you don't start at full capacity. You begin with fewer spoons and narrower margins. *Less cushion for chaos.*

You already know what it means to hit your limit and what happens when you do. The skill regression and the shutdowns. The unthreading of functionality until every decision feels like splinters under the skin.

Last year after Idalia, I kept pushing anyway.

Like trying to hold water in a torn bag patched with peeling tape.

Telling myself I could rest soon. Once we moved, once we found structure again, I would rebuild routine. I told myself familiarity would wrap itself around me like a beloved sweater that had already memorized the shape of my body. *That I could come back to myself.* I wasn't trying to be reckless. I was trying to be careful. Preparing for a huge change with the precision of someone who couldn't afford not to.

I couldn't afford to burn out. But I kept skimming the edge of it. Risking collapse for the sake of forward motion. Until the second flood came and the moment of rest I'd been crawling toward vanished again.

Burnout used to feel like a wave that crashed over me.

It was loud, sudden, and obvious.
Now it feels like erosion.

Like sediment gathering in my worn out joints. Silt in my lungs. A slow leak in the plumbing of my nervous system no one else can hear or see.

It doesn't look like distress anymore. It looks like nothing. Like staring at a wall because I can't remember the steps to get dressed. Like flinching when the microwave beeps, even though I'm the one who pressed start. Like forgetting that eating might help because the idea of chewing feels like too much.

We were never anywhere long enough to get used to anything.

The lights at the rentals were too bright. The sheets were their own unique kind of scratchy on every new bed. The utensils were never quite the right shape. I could barely memorize the new addresses or lock codes before they changed again.

Nothing ever felt the way it was supposed to be.
I needed something to give.

Yet even when people helped, I was still performing. Monitoring everything from how I spoke, how I looked, to how I reacted. Trying not to be too flat or too overwhelmed.

Trying not to be too much of anything.

And when it came time to deal with the systems that were supposed to help, like disaster relief organizations, the insurance adjusters and the county, I had to regulate my tone, my posture, and my face. Perform normalcy with facial muscles that no longer understood how to properly smile on command.

I had no idea what my face was supposed to do after our house flooded again. So I made it do what I thought they needed to see. All the while, the noise didn't stop. Not just the literal noise, the fans, the traffic, the dogs barking behind every rental's fence,

but the noise inside my body.

The pressure. The static.
Like my skin was trying to scream through me.

Most people think of sensory overload as a sudden bang. A loud party. Too many blinking lights. But it's not always dramatic. Sensory overload doesn't always arrive like a storm.

Sometimes it's drywall dust clinging to your eyelashes while a layer of sweat slowly accumulates all over your face and body. It can be calcifying under the moisture. A slow-drip disintegration of tolerance.

Until the wrong spoon touches your lips and makes you flinch. Until your new shirt still has a tag you forgot to cut off and feels like it's slicing you open. Until food doesn't just taste wrong, it feels wrong, and stays on your tongue like regret. And you can't seem to force yourself to swallow. Until sound feels like a punch. Until someone's kindness feels like a demand.

You think you just need sleep. *A day to reset.* But rest doesn't reach the places where you've been scraping yourself raw.

I used to explain these things.
Now I don't.

Not because I don't want to be understood, but due to no longer having the energy or desire to translate my pain into something palatable. Tired of softening the language when my body still carries the tension.

Autistic burnout isn't just a response to stress. It's what happens when your strategies for appearing "fine" finally collapse. When the mask you were wearing to interact with the world around you, fuses to your skin and starts to rot.

You feel it.

But taking it off would hurt worse. So you keep it on, the best you can. You keep smiling and folding laundry. Keep articulately replying to emails with the right amount of exclamation points. Until one day, you can't. And still, somewhere inside the collapse, I began to miss things. Not the house itself. But the pieces of it that overstimulated me in familiar ways.

The sanded grout lines on our kitchen floor. Their roughness created a textured map I could use to feel exactly where I was. The hum of the refrigerator at night. The burnt smell the oven made if I forgot to clean the drip tray. The floor transitions in the hallway which made the vacuum rattle. The dryer's abrupt little song that never matched the mood. The overhead fans rustling the baby hairs on my neck. The chemical tang of bug spray in the corners during summer. The window blinds that clicked in the wind like a nervous habit the house couldn't break.

Even the chairs which were lumpy and overused,
knew how to hold me.

I missed crawling into my bed when the world got too prickly.

My nest of blankets.
My headphones.
My worn-out clothes.

Some of them I'd had since high school.

They were trustworthy on my skin.

I missed the things I knew, even the ones that once made me flinch because at least they were ours. That was home. Not always comfort, but familiar discomfort. Noise I had learned to trust. Textures I could move around in. A rhythm I didn't have to think too much about.

That's the trick of survival, isn't it? You learn to organize your pain into categories:

The known hurts.
The unknown ones.

The ones you'd do anything to avoid and the ones you'd give anything to get back.

I didn't just lose a house. I lost the silence between known sounds. I lost the permission to let my body rest inside them. And no matter how strong I looked on the outside, how composed or organized I seemed... internally, I was splintering.

You can only carry that for so long.
You can only pretend regulation for so long,
before it costs something more permanent.

34.

Through Screens

It was around the time I stopped believing the emails would lead to anything. When everything was quiet in the worst way. My friend Riham always seemed to know the right time to call me.

I've been friends with Riham for over thirteen years. We met working for a translation company. She in Egypt, me in the United States. Two women on different continents, opposite time zones, sometimes opposite worlds.

When my son was still a baby, she would tell me stories about her daughter. I remember her describing how she shielded her child during the sound of war outside her window. Not metaphorically. Physically.

Tying her body around her daughter's so she could absorb what the world tried to send through the walls. For a while communication was spotty through widespread electricity blackouts in her country. Over and over I would count the moments with bated breath until connection was reestablished.

We've always lived different lives. But somehow, they've bent in the same direction.

Two women. Navigating motherhood, marriage, trauma, and re-invention.

Navigating survival.

There were years we couldn't hold ourselves together, so we held space for each other instead. She reminded me who I was when I forgot. I did the same for her.

It's funny, we've never actually met, not in person. However, I could tell you how her cheeks lift when she's trying not to smile too wide. I can explain to you the exact shape her brows make when she's disappointed or frustrated. There's a kind of knowing that lives beyond geography. *We earned that.*

In the last two years, we've been rebuilding together. Not the same structures, not the same ground, but the same mission. I held tools, building permits and insurance forms. She held work timesheets, identification forms and immigration paperwork. We waited. We fought for places to call home. For lives worth stepping into.

She was preparing to move to a new country. I was trying to rebuild a house that barely stood. Nevertheless at the core, we were the same.

Mothers.
Stubborn.
Resilient not by choice, but by necessity.

Pushing through every obstacle for the chance at something better for our families.

We had every reason to drift apart. Different cultures, different pressures, different pain. We could have said: You don't understand. But instead we found every reason to stay close.

To keep going.
Together.

Even in our own messes, we made time. Even when the world pulled us in different directions, we chose to reach across it. Not because it was easy. But because some friendships become their own kind of home.

Our check-in calls almost always happen early. It has to be morning for me, the only time we both have slivers of quiet within a time zone difference that tries to keep us divided. My house, still humming with sleep. The air is cool enough to pretend it's gentle. I step outside, sit in a folding chair, and wait for her to ring. On my end the sky is shifting shades behind the trees, slowly lifting itself into day.

When my screen lights up, she's there smiling, wrapped in a sweater. Eyes tired, but still catching light. We talk about everything and nothing. And then everything again. She's navigating bureaucracy that was never built for women like her. Never meant to make room. The visa process is grinding her down. She's homesick, disoriented, floating in a country which hasn't yet decided if it will let her land.

She tells me she feels like she's unraveling. I tell her she's earned that unraveling. She's held so much for so long. It makes perfect sense to be tired.

We talk about how we thought things would look different by now. How we thought the rebuilding would be over. How we both miss versions of home that no longer exist. How we were so tired of trying to start over.

I say, "We're not going back. But maybe we're going forward."

She cries.
I cry.

We don't apologize for it.
There's nothing to apologize for.

And then, like we always do, we laugh. Not to erase the heaviness, but to make space around it. We laugh as resistance, like we still belong to joy, even now.

We swap sarcastic expressions, inside jokes with no setup. We tilt our heads in synchronized disbelief about whatever new absurdity the day has handed us. We remind each other who we are. We remind each other what we've overcome.

When it's time to hang up, we say what we always say. "We got this." "I love you." "I wish we had more time."

But it's always enough. *Somehow, it's always enough.*

One day, we say, we'll be in the same room. Side-by-side. Not screen-to-screen. Not thousands of miles apart. We'll share tea and sunlight and revel in our earned peace. And maybe we will sit together in the disbelief that we finally made it.

For now, this is still showing up. And showing up, even like this, still matters, especially now. Especially when it feels so rare to truly be seen.

The call ended.
The sun has fully risen.

The day ahead still held everything I hadn't figured out.

But for a moment, I was reminded that I wasn't doing it alone. If I could remember the ones who stay despite the weight of it all. The ones who didn't succumb to emotional or physical distance.

35.

The Scam House

It looked decent from the outside.

The rental house sat tucked into a quiet neighborhood. The kind where people still watered their lawns regularly despite the chilly weather. Remnants of the holidays that passed just weeks before still hung on most of the houses in the form of wreaths and string lights.

For the first time in a long time, pulling into a driveway didn't feel like bracing for impact.

We were feeling good. *Relieved, even.*

Temporary, I reminded myself again. Just a few days while we waited for the electrical repairs to be done to the house we had originally booked. *The one closer to home.* A glitch, not a catastrophe.

The entryway was plain, but neat. The windows gleamed under a hard sun. Nothing outwardly screamed danger. We parked, unloaded our bags, punched in the key code, but it didn't work. *Okay small hiccup.* We contact the property manager, get the correct code and enter the front door.

The smell wafts towards us before the door even swung all the way back. Dog urine, laced with the sharp chemical bite of failed cover-ups. It caught in the back of our noses, made our eyes sting. My husband glanced at me over the kids' heads, a quick flash of let's just get through this.

Inside, the house looked fine if you didn't breathe too deeply or look too closely. The furniture seemed new but somehow tired. The floors were warped under the area rugs. And everywhere, seeping up through the walls, pooling in the air, was that smell.

But we were exhausted.
And tired people make compromises.

The second night, while setting up the beds, my husband crouched down to check the master bed frame.

"There's something under here," he said, voice flat.

A diaper. Or what had once been a diaper. Hardened, shrunken, fossilized with old poop, wedged against the wall under the bed.

I pressed my hand against my forehead, pressing the reaction down like a migraine. *Temporary*, I told myself again. We can fix it. We had already fixed worse.

We stripped the bedding immediately. As the sheets peeled back, more things appeared. A soiled sock tangled between the mattress and frame. Pink mold stains flowering across the pillowcases. When we washed them, we found more. Pillows with the same discoloration. The faint chemical scent of something trying and failing to be sanitized.

Small issues. Not enough to make a fuss.

We bought new pillows that night. New towels too, the ones here were stained or tattered or missing completely. There were no kitchen towels. The coffee maker harbored black and white mold inside its reservoir and old grinds.

We kept adding to the list:

There were no toiletries.

One of the stove's burners didn't work.

The fridge reeked.

The TV didn't have a cord.

The toilet seat slid off because it was only half attached.

A coffee mug fell apart and cut my hand when I filled it.

There were holes that looked to be punched or kicked through doors.

The HVAC heat wouldn't turn on for 12 days and the property manager didn't have a sense of urgency to get it fixed. Despite the 30 degree temperatures outside.

The electric fireplace in the study and the space heaters we brought to try to stay warm, overloaded the breakers if we dared plug in a laptop in another room at the same time.

The list continued to grow.

We patched the gaps ourselves. Buying what we could, cleaning what we couldn't replace. We tried to keep the kids busy, distracted and detached. But it was the little things fraying us. It was death by a thousand small insults.

The insects dead along the baseboards. The mayflies bouncing off our faces as we tried to sleep. The bloody noses our daughter started getting after breathing inside the house for five days straight. The way the porch windows stayed cracked open, hiding the dog urine smell under the excuse of "fresh air."

And then there was the refund.

When the property manager, Tanya, first told us about the electrical issues at our original booking, she asked us to cancel the VRBO reservation ourselves. So it wouldn't hurt her host record. We agreed. It was in good faith. Believing we'd be moved in a few days, as soon as repairs were done.

Days passed.
No updates.

Every time we asked about the electrical fix, Tanya promised she was checking and would update us by the end of the day. Most days, she didn't.

Meanwhile, the refund never came. When I called VRBO myself, they told me no refund had been processed on Tanya's end. *Not even initiated.* She had promised she was "working on it." Promised she had "put it through." Promised she was "just waiting for it to clear."

All lies.

In the end, I had to do the legwork myself. I filed the dispute. Chased down the case number. Attached the screenshots of all our communication I insisted be typed out in texts. I documented every promise she made and broke. I knew, even exhausted, even desperate, that like everything else, nobody would care unless I had proof.

The money mattered. We were drowning under the weight of rental fees, hotel stays, rebuying necessities and paying for a house we couldn't inhabit. Every dollar mattered.

I didn't have the luxury of hoping for the best.
I had to force it.

Tanya also kept promising to send a maintenance crew. Every morning we scrambled. I would rush an hour back from our broken house after tearing out drywall and cleaning left over mud-soaked debris. Just to sit inside the rental, waiting. Waiting for a knock which never came.

Panic creeping higher each time I checked the clock. Worried we'd miss them somehow. Maybe my husband was on a call and I had been in the shower. We were afraid if we left for even an hour, we'd lose our only chance to have something fixed.

Day after day, no one showed. Finally, near the last week and a half of our stay, someone came. A contractor. Not for us, it turned out. He was there to measure for renovations that would begin after we left, new floors, new baseboards, new drywall.

He didn't know who Tanya was. He didn't know about our heating issues or the mold or the broken appliances. He wasn't there to fix anything for us. He was there to erase us and all the previous tenants, the second we were gone.

I kept telling myself it wasn't personal.

Maybe it was just bad luck.
Maybe they were overwhelmed too.
Maybe they didn't mean to let everything rot.

But some small, stubborn part of me, the part that hadn't drowned yet, whispered *keep documenting*. Keep protecting yourselves. Don't stop writing it all down.

... Just in case.

Just in case it wasn't incompetence.
Just in case it was something worse.

We stayed. On the grounds that, what else could we do? There were no other options. We had already burned through every favor, every dollar, every reasonable alternative.

Temporary, I reminded myself again. Stacking each new insult on top of the last.

Temporary.

We stayed for three weeks. Waiting, hoping, documenting. Breathing in the rot and trying to believe it wasn't deliberate. Trying to believe we hadn't traded one kind of struggle for another.

***

Almost two months later I'd see her name in a Facebook post warning local renters about a scam. My chest tightened before I even opened the comments. Tanya. Not just a Tanya, *the* Tanya.

The one who had booked us into that house... The one with carpets soaked in urine. Bleach trying and failing to cover the odor and an overwhelming sense something was very, very wrong. I clicked anyway, *even though I already knew*. And there it was.

She hadn't been a real property manager at all. Just a receptionist at a legitimate property management company. She had allegedly taken advantage of her access. Copied inactive listings and created her own rental scheme. She'd been placing desperate families like ours in houses she didn't own or truly manage. Collecting money through a personal bank account she created using the real company's name. Then moving on to her next target before anyone caught on. *She even provided company invoices.*

The comment section read like a choir of exhausted disbelief.

Every voice echoed some version of our story. Families misled, placed in the wrong house, told to be patient. Most people hadn't reported it. They assumed it was their own mistake or figured there was nothing to be done. I almost didn't report it either. At the time, I thought I was just being difficult. *Paranoid even.* A little too sensitive to a bad smell and a confusing handoff of key codes.

But now I knew it wasn't just us.

The owner of the company had initiated the thread herself. Trying to track down victims. I messaged her. She replied to me that same day. I could tell, from the moment she started talking, she hadn't been prepared for the scope of what Tanya had done.

It wasn't her listing, but it was her company's name that had been used to bait us. Tanya had worked there. She knew how to make it look legitimate. The owner was stunned. Horrified. She apologized over and over. Not because she had done anything personally, but because she recognized what it meant to be the unaware final link, in a chain that had let people get hurt.

She asked if I had documentation.
I told her I had everything.

Screenshots of every message, the receipts, the hosting site's refund claim, the names of the maintenance people Tanya sent to "fix" things. I even had phone records and photos. At the time, I hadn't saved those things with any clear plan. I just didn't trust my memory. I was so used to being told I was exaggerating, misremembering, making it worse than it was. I needed evidence, not for a court case but for myself. To anchor the story in something no one could rewrite later.

She told me I had more proof than anyone else they'd spoken to. A detective was already involved. A criminal case had been opened. The number of victims was still growing.

Then she told me something that made my stomach twist. Tanya was also under investigation for FEMA fraud. She had accepted rental assistance from people who had nowhere else to go. People like us. I didn't know if our partial reimbursement was connected to that specific rental. But I wasn't going to wait to find out. I contacted FEMA immediately. Explained the situation. They flagged the file and told me they'd investigate on their end.

It should have felt like justice. I should have felt powerful or at least relieved being able to hand over so much evidence. Yet all I could think was, we still lived there. We still breathed the air. My kids still walked through the house gagging on the smell. I still laid out blankets over a bed that made me feel dirty, no matter how many times we laundered the sheets.

Being right hadn't protected us. It hadn't prevented anything.

It had only confirmed what I already suspected. *I had no one to rely on but myself and my own exhausted instincts. And even they didn't always keep us safe in time.*

Even after the interaction with the company owner, I kept waiting for something to go wrong. That Tanya might disappear. The homeowner might change his mind and somehow blame us for being there at all and dragging him into this mess.

That's what this does to you.

It rewires your expectations. I didn't feel vindicated. I felt exposed. Like I'd given someone else the map to my survival, and now I had to hope they wouldn't use it against me.

I kept the photos of the rental. The case number. The list of names. Just in case someone needed proof again. *Just in case I did.*

36.

No Good Choices Left

The smell of another rental hits us the second we walk in, the way it usually does when we arrive somewhere unfamiliar. The way we keep wishing it wouldn't this time.

This time it wasn't sharp, not exactly fresh, just old. An accumulation of multiple tenants, with multiple pets, with no maintenance for who knows how long. It sunk deep into the walls and the carpets and the air ducts. Surging into the rooms every time the AC kicked on. They replaced the air filter the next day and told us it was fixed. It isn't. It lingers under everything. Despite the deodorizer sprays, air fresheners and candles we bought. Even after opening the windows and doors, it is still there.

The kitchen is worse than the last one. Not missing as many things or broken. But grimy utensils with crusted food stuck on the handles, sticky counters and sticky floors. Everything had a layer of residue and stains.

In the bathroom the toilet tips over to one side when one of us sits on it. We realize it hasn't been properly bolted down and there is a small leak from the seam.

It's not one thing. It's the thousand small insults layering over each other, until they become unbearable.

Our daughter's room is a converted den with a fold-out couch, broken, half-collapsing and stained. The first night, giant palmetto bugs climb out from under the furniture. Fat, slow, and gleaming. She refuses to sleep there afterwards. Won't even step barefoot on the floor. I bring back an air mattress and she drags it into her brother's room.

Part of me wants to tell her it's fine. We'll fix it. We'll make it work. But my mouth won't form the words because she's right. I'm tired of lying to both of us.

***

At some point, in the middle of the afternoon, I open my notebook and laptop. I review our finances and our budget. Over $20,000 spent on short-term housing within five months. We can't afford another rental. I stare at the numbers and wonder if it's too late to recoup some of the cost. I remembered last year we were offered a month's worth of rental reimbursement from FEMA. This time, it didn't trigger because Greg's job covered housing at first. I didn't want to double dip. I didn't appeal the denial. We thought we wouldn't need it.

Just a few more weeks of lodging. *Then we'd have answers. Then we'd have a plan.*

But a few weeks turned into a month. Then another. Then a few more weeks. Then more waiting. And now, all of a sudden, it was already February.

But the money ran out a while ago. Our savings dwindled faster than we could adjust and our credit cards were on the verge of being maxed out. I researched nonprofits and community programs. We didn't qualify. *I knew that already.* We existed in the in-between. More stable than some. But not stable enough to keep financing two lives. One keeping a damaged house running, the other in limbo.

Not after last year.

I minimized the spreadsheet I had been rebuilding. Our property contents breakdown, the one the adjuster just requested, again. He said if I formatted it just so, if I lined it up exactly with the photos in the coinciding folder, he might be able to expedite his side. It didn't matter that I had sent my original list only weeks after the storm. That I'd already done this. *Twice.*

I reopened the FEMA website. Reread the section about rental assistance. I already knew the limits wouldn't match the cost of housing during a disaster. Not with price gouging. Not with availability shrinking. But even a fraction was more than we had.

So I packed up my paperwork and drove to the local Ace Hardware where FEMA had set up a help desk.

I'd been to this store many times before. It was smaller than the big box stores. *But it felt safer.*

Here, no one questioned me when I hoisted heavy bags of mortar into my cart. No one asked where my husband was or why he had sent me to the store. No one "little lady-ed" me or tried to place their hand on my back. No one tried to explain my projects to me. I wasn't patronized like I had shown up with a Pinterest project and no plan for its execution.

I was just a person shopping for materials.

Nothing more.
Nothing less.

Inside, I found two men seated at a folding table. One was from FEMA. One was from my flood insurance provider. I explained my situation. How we had been trying to stay afloat. How we were running out of room to do so.

The FEMA rep made a call. He got through within minutes. *I had spent hours on those same phone lines.* He initiated a request and logged my details. He said I'd have a response within a week.

The insurance guy hands me flyers I had already memorized months ago. Still, I nodded politely. He asked questions. At first, I thought maybe he could help. I explained the spreadsheets, the contractor quotes, the rebuilds. I asked how we were supposed to sell a home with an open claim and a mortgage. He didn't know. He had guesses. But so did I, *and I was hoping for something more.*

He tried to pivot to housing tips.

"Maybe try to buy somewhere outside a flood zone next time," he suggested.

I smiled so I wouldn't snarl. Laughed it off like it was a new idea. As if I hadn't just spent the last twenty minutes telling him that was the goal. That was the plan.

He continued with construction advice. "Have you considered..." "Did you know..."

I didn't want to have to prove I belonged at this table too *but I could feel it already starting.* Because I had, I had considered all of it. But I swallowed the explanations I wanted to throw back at him. I was trying not to shrink too much, while also trying not to snap.

Mid-sentence, he interrupts me.
"What did you go to school for?"

"Mathematics," I said, gently.

"Oh. So you're actually really smart."

ACTUALLY!

As if it was a revelation. As if intelligence had to be earned through disclosure.

I'm pretty sure it was meant as a compliment. Maybe even validation. But the subtext on this was not lost on me.

And like too many of us "actually" smart women do, I continue to play nice. I continued the rest of the conversation as if it would be fruitful. Then I shook his hand and thanked him for the help.

They told me where they'd be next week in case I needed more support.

"Thanks." I said. "I'll keep that in mind."

...And I will.
I'll keep it in mind, so I don't go there next week!

***

When I returned to the rental, I updated Greg and Landon. I skipped over most of the frustrating parts but I let one thing slip. They both rolled their eyes. *Not at me. At the world.* In that "not again" kind of way.

Landon has already offered to go with me on errands. To be a buffer. Even at twelve, he understands his presence changes how I'm treated.

I tell him "it's okay."
Well. Not okay, but I'm used to it.

"You can't come with me every time I have to go out in public. This is just the way it goes sometimes."

I ask only that he remembers this. That he grows up knowing what it looks like and chooses not to replicate it.

"When it's your turn, do better." I say.

And I know he will.

***

Four days later, I received confirmation of two months of partial rental reimbursement. It's not enough but it's something. I can apply to extend it, but I know already that it won't stop the hemorrhaging of our bank account.

Around the same time, maybe even the same day, the toilet overflows. Not just a little. A full surge. Water spilling into the bathroom, bleeding under the wall toward the kitchen, threatening to swamp the whole side of the house.

I hear myself yell to the kids before I even think. "Lift everything!" The words slice out of me. Sharp. Automatic. *Too familiar.* The kids scramble, grabbing backpacks, shoes, and hoisting Fay's air mattress onto Landon's bed to get it off the ground. *I've said this before...*

Why are we bleeding ourselves dry just to relive the same moments of panic we were trying to avoid?

This isn't safety.
This isn't rest.

This isn't much better, honestly. I bite down hard against the rising bile. *At least our broken home is ours. At least the floors that flood are ours to mop.*

The owner doesn't call a plumber. She sends her parents and their friend to "investigate." They wander the house like tourists, squinting at damp baseboards, flipping the toilet handle, mumbling to each other. The dad says something about a towel. Something about "kids flushing things they shouldn't." It's an accusation wrapped in a folksy shrug. My husband tries to explain that our children know better than to flush the towel the couple found. That we were homeowners and our kids were educated on how to take care of a house. That they would never jeopardize our lodging with such an inconsiderate action. But it didn't matter.

It doesn't seem like they want to hear it. We try not to react. Not out loud at least.

Inside, I am already packing us up again. Inside, I am already choosing the broken walls of our own house over this slow-burn humiliation.

We stay one night in a hotel while they "fix" it. Refunded for the inconvenience. As if a single night refund could bleach the smell out of our skin. When we come back, the rug is damp and the air is thicker than before. We quickly realize the suspected water damage we had found in the kitchen after moving in, probably wasn't from a storm flood cover up. *It started to seem like this had definitely happened before.*

A few days later, the toilet backs up again! We catch it early this time. Not a flood, just a warning. We don't even say anything out loud anymore. We just lift everything instinctively, muscle memory from the last time and the time before that.

Because some lessons, once learned, never leave your bones.

We are out of places to go.
Out of rentals.
Out of money.
Out of second chances.

Moving back into the gutted house isn't a choice anymore. It's survival. It's the only place where the walls, even if they are broken, unfinished and water-stained, at least don't lie to us. We gather the kids. We load the car. We go home.

If it even still counts as that.

37.

Asymptote

So here's a poetic unpacking of an "actually smart" mathematics term.
This one's for you, Mr. Insurance Guy.

You wanted credentials.
I gave you strategy.
Now I'll give you a metaphor.

In mathematics, an asymptote describes a line on a graph and the behavior of a curve as it stretches toward infinity.
It gets closer and closer to the fixed line but never touches.

Take the function $f(x) = 1/x$.
As x increases, the graph gets closer and closer to the x-axis
It approaches y=0, continuously.

The values and distance shrinks by fractions so small you almost can't see them.

But contact never happens.
Not even at the end.
Since there is no end.
The curve continues infinitely.

And sometimes I wonder...
Was this always going to go on forever?

Is this what we're in now?
A kind of infinite approach?

No landing.
No resolution.
Just endless recalculations.

There is motion.
There is effort.
But there is no arrival.

I used to think we were moving toward something. A version of life where things would finally click into place. Where we'd have decisions made, paperwork finalized, and plans locked down. Where we'd feel steady again, even if we didn't call it safe.

But what we had was not the movement we strived for. *Not really.*

It was calculation.
Contingencies.
Constant rewrites of our "next step" based on what might happen next week, what might clear, what might break.

We were living in a math problem with too many variables.
And no real answer key.

People asked, "So where are you guys at now?" I didn't know how to answer without a paragraph.

Waiting on insurance.
Waiting on housing.
Waiting on job approvals.

Waiting to know if we were allowed to leave or expected to rebuild again in a place that had already undone us twice.

It wasn't stuck exactly.
It just wasn't forward in big noticeable ways.
We weren't spiraling anymore.
But we weren't landing either.

That's when I started thinking about asymptotes. Not as a metaphor for healing. *That would come later.* But as a way to explain the sensation of almost.

The idea that if we just waited a little longer, we'd finally touch the thing we kept hovering near.

But I know how asymptotes work. They close in.
They look like they may converge.
But they never touch.

Maybe we were meant to get close, not done.
Maybe this season wasn't about arrival.
Maybe it was about tolerating proximity,
without demanding certainty.

Because that's the thing about a curve and an asymptote,

it just gets harder to see the space left
between almost and never.

And that's where we were.
In the decimal place between crisis and clarity.
Still bending toward something,
we weren't sure we'd ever be allowed to reach.

38.

Wind Driven

It was held at the Civic Club. Where Landon had attended summer camp. Where Fay's art and yoga classes were. The same room where they once distributed boxes of donated diapers, Clorox wipes, and nonperishables. I remembered the folding tables lined with supplies, the signs taped to walls, the flood survivors scanning the bins for sizes and dignity.

Now five months after Helene, I was here looking for answers.

The seminar was hosted by a nonprofit I had connected my neighbor Steve with months earlier. I had brought him in when he wasn't sure where to go. That's how I met the host, a case manager working with the locals. She had helped him get enrolled. And when I walked in, she recognized me.

I wasn't here just for myself. She knew I was here for neighbors too. To collect flyers, handouts, and resource lists. I already knew I didn't qualify for everything in the folder, but I knew who might. *I was learning to carry paperwork like first aid supplies, not always for me, but still urgent to collect and important to disperse.*

I also had a personal question. I had called various legal aids, researched everything I could find, but no one could give me a straight answer about our situation. Not about the house, and not about my husband's job. I was hoping one of the attorneys here might.

The room was full. People had driven from all over the county. Some came from neighboring counties.

Everyone here had lost something.

They handed out folders with printouts and checklists. I opened mine, underlining the sections I didn't already know. The speakers were kind. Practical. They talked about FEMA appeals, insurance denials, community assistance, the technicalities of wind-driven water. I took notes, watching the crowd closely.

Hands started going up.
The questions came in waves.

"Why isn't this covered?"
"Can you help me?"
"Who can?"
"What are we supposed to do next?"

"I lost my house," someone said. "This is the second time."

You could feel the air tighten. The room was full of people who needed help, and the people at the front were doing their best. But I could hear the frustration behind every question. I could feel the desperation threading through every pause.

Then, somewhere behind me, a sound broke the tension.

A long, unmistakable fart.
Not delicate. Not ignorable.

Two rows back, someone had surrendered to biology. The room stuttered into stillness. No one reacted. No one even acknowledged it. Everyone sat perfectly still. Like maybe we could all pretend it hadn't happened.

I glanced around. Caught eyes with the couple next to me. *My face is definitely saying without words "you heard that too, right?"* The man to my left began to rub his forehead. His shoulders started to shake with laughter. I looked down, sucked my lips in between my teeth, and pressed my palm into my face trying desperately not to join him. He was folding into himself now, trying so hard to hold the laughter in. *But he couldn't.*

None of us really could hold it all in any longer.

And maybe that was the point.
There are only so many things you can hold in.

Your fear.
Your exhaustion.
Your questions.
Your grief.

The air inside your body.
Eventually, something gets out.

39.

The Weight of Waiting

By the end of February, we were back in the house.
Back in the frame of it, anyway.

The walls inside were still bare studs in most places. Plastic stapled up
to keep the dust down and provide a little privacy in the bedrooms
and bathroom. No real furniture yet. Just a few folding tables, air
mattresses, and weathered chairs we had managed to clean enough to
use again, which creaked when you sat too fast.

It didn't feel like home, but it didn't feel catastrophic anymore either. It
felt like something in between. A strange, suspended kind of life.

When we first moved back in, I put up curtain rods and curtains in
all the bedroom and bathroom doorways for privacy. It worked for a
couple of days but they kept falling on our heads every few days when
we walked through. So I switched to stapling magnetic draft door
coverings to the door frames. It's not pretty, but it's practical. It's the
solution you settle for when you're living somewhere that's not quite a
construction site, but not quite a home either.

***

Two months into living here, the house still didn't feel right. *But it*
didn't feel like a disaster zone anymore.

We tried to keep pretending we actually believed it was temporary.

But some things gave us away. Friends and neighbors brought over extra furniture. Side tables, cabinets, dressers, and a headboard. The kinds of things you need if you're staying somewhere longer than you planned.

Loading our clothes into those dressers felt heavier than I expected. Hanging sweaters in the closet felt like surrender. Not because we wanted to give up, but because we couldn't keep living week to week, pretending life was about to change any second.

The suitcases we had lived out of for months finally got unpacked. For the first time in nearly half a year, our clothes weren't stuffed in wrinkled piles, dragged from place to place.

It felt wrong, somehow.
Relieving, and wrong.

We cooked meals on a hotplate, in a gifted Instant Pot, on a grill borrowed from neighbors and in our old microwave we were able to salvage. The old stove was long gone, ripped out with the flood-soaked cabinets, and we didn't replace it. A dorm sized fridge sits in its old place. A fridge a quarter of the size of the one it was replacing.

It took over a half hour to boil a pot of water for making a family worth of pasta on the cheap hotplate we bought. That was over 30 minutes just to get it to boil before actually placing the pasta in to cook it! We learned we can use an electric kettle we had saved, to boil water in small quantities and mix it into the pot to speed things along.

Once my husband bought frozen pizzas because we were too tired to cook. Only to realize we had forgotten we don't own an oven to cook them in. We had to cut each frozen pizza into slices. Placing each piece into the small air-frier we repurchased. It ended up taking over an hour and way more effort than planned, to cook "the easy dinner."

We laughed about it afterward.

But it was laughter adjacent to crying.

What was the point of buying another stove though? If we were leaving soon, it would be a waste. If we were still here when hurricane season circled back, it would be another heartbreak. It would become just another item on an insurance personal property loss spreadsheet again.

Everything we did came with a mental asterisk.

*But just for now**
*But just until**

A friend even bought us a second work sink so we could stop using the utility sink we had dragged in from the garage as part of our temporary kitchen, as also part of our bathroom routine. One sink in the house had worked technically, for all intents and purposes. But there's something about washing dishes in the same basin where you brushed your teeth and washed your face, that never stopped feeling wrong.

Never stopped reminding us, this wasn't how life was supposed to be lived.

***

When I first put plastic on the walls, we used thick frosted-like plastic, thinking it would give us some privacy. Then I realized it's see-through when you turn the light on to use the bathroom once the sun goes down. We switched to black plastic.

Even our privacy had to be learned the hard way.

Don't get me started on the lack of soundproofing when there's missing drywall.

Eventually, I put up a single mirror in the house. It was the first time I'd seen myself properly in a while. I don't actually know how long it had been. I think I used my phone's front facing camera to pick something out of my teeth at one point.

Two rentals ago, I had found my first full grey hair. Now I have three more right beside it. The mirror reflected more than just my face. It reflected time passing, stress accumulating, and a version of myself I barely recognized.

Most of what we salvaged still sits packed away in bins. We didn't want to unpack any of it. It felt safer to keep it sealed. Like maybe if we didn't lay claim to this place again, we could still leave when the time came.

Every time I needed something, a shirt, a ladle, a notebook and pen, I had to dig through the bins. Sifting, rooting, and apologizing to myself in my head.

We didn't want to fully unpack.
We didn't want to fully stay.

Every once and a while I'd find something I thought we had saved. Something we tried to clean in hopes of keeping, but was now taken over by mold and contaminating the things packed next to it. It became another reason not to unpack.

I'd rather store things we had actually lost, if it meant we could keep the delusion a little longer.

Our living room doesn't have a couch. Instead, we set up three hammocks we used to tie between trees outside. We put them on metal stands spread out like a campsite indoors. It's economical. It's fun, if you squint at it right.

It gets the job done.

But I miss the feeling of sinking into cushions. The way a real couch makes a house feel inhabited, not just survived. The hammocks are fine.

Everything is fine.

Fine in that brittle way you can survive on for a while.

And then there's the dust. No matter how much I sweep, mop, vacuum, or wipe, it keeps coming back. Where it comes from, I don't know. It seeps out of the open studs, rides the air like a second skin. If I skip even a day, you can see the particles dancing in the sunbeams that sneak through the windows, twirling like they're mocking me.

It never stops.

It never lets the house feel clean.
It never lets us forget the damage we're living inside.

The kids' air mattresses are holding on by a thread too. Every time we patch one leak, another hissing sound appears a few nights later. Quiet at first, barely noticeable except for the slow softening of the bed under their bodies. Each dab of glue and patch buys a little more time. Nothing more.

It feels like living on borrowed hours.

The type of repairs you make when you can't quite afford to start over, but you can't quite afford to let go either.

It feels odd not to be rebuilding this year. After the demo and major cleaning was done and we had moved back in, there was still so much to fill my days. Yet, I felt like I wasn't accomplishing anything. At least when I was building I could see progress. I could touch it. But now, no matter how proactive I am, it feels like I'm just waiting for others to determine our fate.

I have to fight the urge to put up wallboard.
I think about how easy it could be just to start fixing things.

To do something, even if I would have to rip it out again.

The tools I need, *well at least most of them that survived*, are right there in the garage. On a high shelf, along with the left over drywall seam tape from last year. The studs are exposed and waiting. It would be so simple to hang drywall, to make the walls solid again.

We're still trying to be strategic. With our time, our effort, our money. *It's still a tightrope balancing act.* Every choice feels like a gamble still. Spend too much settling, and we might lose it all again. Spend too little, and we're just suffering needlessly.

We try to bring in slivers of normalcy.

We set up TVs so the kids can zone out for a while, feel something close to regular life. We set up our son's computer desk. Not because it made sense, but because it gave him a place to feel anchored. Playing his video games the way he used to before the flood turned everything into moving parts.

We reluctantly unpacked our daughter's additional craft supplies. Boxes of markers, paper, paintbrushes scattered across a folding table.

It felt dangerous.
Dangerous, to be investing in joy.

But watching her sit there, laser-focused, entirely absorbed in creating something new, for a little while, the house didn't feel like a ruin. In those brief flickering moments, it feels like a home again.

We've become a whole new level of adaptable.

No more bouncing from rental to rental, stuffing the car with essentials, ratchet-strapping suitcases to the trailer hitch like vagabonds with nowhere left to run. No more waiting for another stranger's Wi-Fi password, another scratchy set of sheets, another apology about the smell, the stains, the broken appliances, the bugs.

Now the house is ours again.

Ours, and still wrecked.
Ours, and still temporary.

A home suspended between what was and what could be, but neither something we wanted anymore. We want out. Not a life rebuilt on top of dust that never settles.

We knew we should make the best of it. To live in the present while waiting for the future. Be grateful for the options we did have.

Anchor ourselves, even if only lightly. But how do you balance hope with stability, without choking on one or the other? If we buy a real couch, are we saying we gave up on leaving? If we hang pictures on the walls, are we giving up on the dream of a better home away from here?

And yet, if we don't...

If we keep living out of boxes, keep sleeping on borrowed time, keep holding our breath, what kind of life are we modeling for our kids?

Our children are tired too. I can see it in the way they hesitate before making plans. I can see it in the way their eyes dull when we talk about "someday." They want something real. Something now.

If I can't convince them to hold out hope any longer, maybe the best thing I can do is help them find joy in what we have. Let them have friends over. Let them walk down and sit on the dock to feel the sun on their faces. Let them hang decorations on their walls, even if the studs are still exposed.

Even if it's all temporary.
Even more so, because it's all temporary.

It's not giving up. It's refilling the empty cups we've been running on for far too long.

The truth is, we don't know how long we'll be here. We don't know how long we'll be waiting. We need to stop holding our breath long enough to actually live.

The flood took so much already.
It doesn't get to take everything.

40.

Lost and Found

I found a message in my spam folder.

Most of what landed there lately was useless, but this one was different. It was from the theater manager in Massachusetts. She said she remembered my post in a local community group from months ago. And someone had just turned in a ring they found. She thought it might be mine. *She hoped it was mine.*

My heart dropped. Not in a bad way, but in a dizzy, too-fast way, when your body doesn't know whether to prepare for disaster or relief. I braced myself.

I hadn't let myself hope. I'd already mourned the ring like it was gone. We'd searched. So many people had searched, staff, strangers, my husband and I and the kids. The theater had swept between rows and checked under seat cushions. I figured it was lost for good. Maybe, someone found it and decided to pawn it or keep it for themselves.

It was spring now. Maybe the snow had melted and revealed what we couldn't find. I didn't ask where or how it ended up in the lost and found.

She sent a photo. And I knew it instantly. Not from the diamond or the setting, although those were familiar. *But that wasn't the proof.* I knew it because of what clung to it. There were still tiny fragments of debris trapped under the bent prongs. Dust and specks of mortar and drywall mud from the house. From the demo. My ring hadn't just been found. It had carried the wreckage with it. Proof that it was still mine. *That it had survived alongside us.*

The theater offered to mail it back free of charge. I thanked her again and again. But I didn't know how to explain what it truly meant to me.

Not really.

It felt like something had broken through. Like the universe had let a thread hold. Something small and precious had made it out. But even that didn't land clean. I didn't know how to do good news anymore. I kept waiting for it to disappear again. Possibly get lost in the mail, on its way back to me. Gratitude and suspicion lived side by side in me by then.

The ring arrived a few days later. I held it in my palm and tried to feel what I was supposed to feel.

Closure.
Relief.
Hope.

And yes. There was a flicker of something close to joy.
Not pure, not full, but real and unexpected.

I posted an update to the Massachusetts group, the one where I'd pleaded for help finding it. I hadn't expected much when I first wrote it. Just a last grasp at something already gone. But now, they celebrated with me from over a thousand miles away. Dozens of congratulatory comments and expressions of relief from people who had searched or shared or simply remembered the post.

It wasn't just a ring anymore. It was a shared victory. A reminder that sometimes, when everything else fails, strangers can still choose to care.

It's the little wins that help me keep pushing through lately.
And this was a big one.

41.

King of the Hollow Castle

In the spirit of narrative fairness, I thought it only appropriate to include a chapter from the most silently judgmental member of our household: our cat, Zipper.

I have been relocated against my will no fewer than seven times. Each time, I was placed inside a metal death trap on wheels. I screamed the entire way. My humans did not seem to enjoy this. They tried everything: soft carriers, towels, blankets and even letting me roam free. Once, they even held me like a baby, whispering comforting things. I screamed into their faces at close range for forty-five straight minutes. Then, for dramatic effect, I farted in one of their laps. They were not comforted.

Ever since the storms, things have been different. They seem... sad. But also obsessed with me. I get extra pets. Extra food ...the good kind. Extra playtime. They talk to me in full sentences. They ask me how I'm doing. I do not respond, but I appreciate the attention.

They're also trying to teach me tricks now. "Touch." and "Give me your paw," they say. If I lift my foot just a little, they hand me a treat and get very excited. I figured it out quickly, but I pretend it's hard. That way, I get more snacks.

At one point they felt guilty for making me live in what they refer to as "the dog pee house," a rental that reeked of other creatures. I didn't like it there. I glared a lot. To make up for it, they bought me a new bed and started taking me on walks.

I am an indoor cat. I was not consulted.

They put me in a harness and clipped on a leash. At first, I refused to walk. I stood perfectly still like a decorative protest statue. Eventually, I gave in. I walked about 100 feet. They celebrated like I had crossed the Alps. They gave me more treats. So now I pretend I don't want to walk, just to get rewarded for "trying."

I am running this show.

Now that we're back in the old house, the one with no walls, life is excellent.

A couple of years ago my humans installed a hallway door to keep me out of their rooms at night. That was adorable. There are no doors now and I can walk between the studs where the walls used to be. I go wherever I want. The hallway is mine now. So is the garage. So is the top of the refrigerator.

In the mornings, I request breakfast before the sun rises. I used to knock gently against the humans and chirp softly. Now I body slam their air mattress and scream into their faces. They must appreciate my enthusiasm, they get out of bed so quickly!

I sleep in their beds, I shed my fur on their pillows, I sit on their laptops and I supervise their sadness. I don't know why they cry sometimes. But when they do, I sit on them. This usually helps.

The humans seem worried about the house. They whisper about mortgages and insurance and "starting over." They spend a lot of time researching things. They move papers from one room to another and then forget where they put them. I try to nap through this part.

The walls may be gone, but my power is growing.

And when the humans left me behind to go to Massachusetts, I was not abandoned. Steve and Lori, the neighbors, became my staff in their absence.

Steve tried to bring me across the street to meet his cat. I declined, politely, but firmly... He returned me to my domain minutes later. Lori made me a catnip toy out of a sock. It was excellent. I accepted it immediately and proceeded to destroy it with great reverence. They are good humans but I was glad when mine came back.

This hollow kingdom is mine now.

And if another storm comes? I will hide in the loft. Then I will emerge, fluffy, victorious and still hungry. Mom said minnows got in last time. Maybe I'll do some fishing.

Because the world is my oyster now.
And I do love seafood.

42.

Fault Lines

For years, I thought my husband's job would be the one thing we could count on. No matter what storms came, literal or figurative, we had that steady paycheck. That government-backed security. That line in the sand I thought we could build a life behind. As long as he worked hard, it was supposed to be safe. Reliable. But like so many things I once trusted, that security turned out to be an illusion.

When our home flooded from Helene, we weren't just fighting the storm's aftermath this time. We were also fighting a new kind of storm. Another new layer of bureaucracy.

I remember sitting in temporary housing, trying to breathe through the weight of it all, while my husband checked his work email again. His jaw tightened with every new message.

Almost every agency was facing potential cuts.

Reductions in force were coming.
Maybe.

Or maybe there'd be a hiring freeze.
Or a benefits slash.
Or all of the above.

No one knew anything for sure. And yet everyone was expected to continue like nothing was happening. Like their entire lives weren't hanging in the balance.

I continued to watch as the stress settled into his bones. Making him smaller. Quieter. He didn't have the energy to talk about it. Not when every ounce of his strength was already spent just trying to hold himself together. And when he did talk about it, there were no words I could offer that didn't feel like lying. *What was I supposed to say?*

It would be okay?
The system would protect us?
Someone would definitely step in?

I had already learned, again and again, help rarely comes from the ones who hold the power.

People assume a federal job means stability. What they don't see are the cracks beneath the surface. They don't see the inbox-refreshing, the rumor-chasing, the way political decisions become personal. How a budget line becomes a broken promise. They don't see what it does to a person, to a family, to never know if the ground beneath them is solid, or if it's already giving way.

And just like in our personal lives, when everything is crumbling, people stand at the edge and nod solemnly. "Let me know if you need anything," they say. "We're all in this together."

Some mean it.
Some don't.

But what could they really do, even if they did?

They aren't in our house at night, watching the light drain slowly from his eyes. They aren't there when he stares at the ceiling, air mattress creaking beneath him, plastic sheeting rustling against the studs where drywall used to be. They don't see the way his mind races long after his body has given out. They aren't lying awake beside him, hoping he doesn't slip away.

Shutdowns.
Hiring freezes.
Budget cuts.

These weren't just headlines to us. They were the difference between rebuilding our life and losing everything again.

When the RIFs (reductions in force) finally started, we held our breath. His name wasn't on the list. *Not this time.*

But it wasn't relief.
It wasn't even a victory.

It was just a temporary reprieve.
Another chance to hold on a little longer.

Another reminder that even when you survive the culling, you're still inside the machine.

And while we feared what was unfolding, there were people cheering for our demise. Some people who knew us were celebrating the restructuring. I wondered if they would feel different if they knew how we were affected. But I continued to bite my tongue in order not to draw attention to us.

And my husband, he kept showing up.
Seeing as, he didn't know how not to.

Even when he was barely sleeping. Even when the house groaned and shifted around us like a wounded animal. Even when all he had left were the broken rhythms of endurance.

Sometimes I'd see him working, headphones on, his laptop perched on a table in a room with no real walls, and I'd feel grief and awe pressed together in the same breath.

He was still achieving.
Still producing.
Still outperforming.

Yet every night, there was less of him left.

He earned an achievement award last year during the aftermath of Idalia. The kind that came with a hard earned reward and provided a much needed sense of validation. It said without saying it, we see you. We value you. The kind of thing that's supposed to symbolize earned stability. What was happening now though, wasn't about merit anymore, despite what was being said.

If it were, we wouldn't be worried.
But we knew the reality was he couldn't afford to slip.

Not once.
Not even a little.

Everything was riding on his ability to perform in a house still held together by tape and breath. *And I hated that.*

I hated how much it cost him to be consistent. I hated how hard I had to work to pretend I wasn't afraid every time he opened his inbox. But most of all, I hated how familiar it all felt.

This endless bracing.
This waiting for the floor to crack again.

So we do what we always do.
We continue to brace.

There's a chance we might be okay, but not bracing means being caught mid-step when the fault line finally moves.

43.

Routine Failure

I start the morning with a plan. Not a perfect one, but a hopeful one.

I stayed up the night before drafting a weekly schedule for the kids. Soft starts with task menus. Space for meltdowns, decompression and play. It was visual, flexible, and familiar. I didn't try to reinvent our lives, just give them shape. I was proud of it in a quiet, cautious way, where pride and dread sit side by side. I knew it wouldn't fix everything, but maybe it would give us all a foothold.

I introduced it to Fay first. She looked at the colors, traced the lines, smiled when she saw her Tuesday art class and Friday yoga. She asked thoughtful questions. She didn't protest. *That in itself felt like a win.*

Then I brought it to Landon.

I barely made it past the words "soft start and breakfast" before he was upset. Said he doesn't want to wake up early. Said he doesn't even eat breakfast. Said we don't have anything good to eat anyway. Even though we have the exact foods he normally eats in the mornings: eggs, bread, strawberries, and cereal. Things he'd requested. *Things I bought because he asked.*

I tried to stay calm. I reminded him that he's been staying up late, past midnight playing games. Maybe, mornings wouldn't feel so hard if he got some sleep. My words came out sharper than I meant, they were tired and short. I watched his expression shift. He rolled his eyes and went quiet. Refusing to participate in further conversation.

I walked away.

Not because I gave up. It was more of the fact that I could feel myself tensing and I didn't want to snap. Not at him. Not when I could tell it wasn't about breakfast at all. *It was about everything.*

Later, I tried again. I told him I could tell things felt hard. I wasn't here to fight. I understood he was overwhelmed. He didn't argue this time. He just deflated.

"When I found out we're stuck here..." he said, "that we're probably not moving anytime soon anymore, I stopped caring. I don't have friends, so who cares if people like me. Nothing means anything. So why should I even try?"

And I broke.

Seeing as, over the last year and a half I've watched almost every one of his friends slip away no matter how much he tried to keep them. Other teenagers don't exactly know what to do with him anymore. They don't know what to say when he's just trying to be honest. They don't have the capacity or fortitude yet to stand by someone going through something like this.

They are kids.
He is still a kid.

And it's not fair, but it's his reality.

I told him the truth. That I desperately want to fix it all, but I don't know how. Sometimes it feels like everything I've done in the last year and a half, trying to protect us, trying to get us out... it hasn't worked. I tell him how I get lonely too. That's why I stay up late writing things no one is going to see. I understand, because sometimes it feels like nothing I do matters too.

I see a lot of myself in Landon sometimes. The way he retreats to the inner workings of his mind. The way he has the natural instinct to file his feelings away. The way he watches the world around him and calculates how to move through it.

I don't tell him this to downplay what he's feeling. *I actually feel guilty for pulling the curtain back.* I remind him that my feelings aren't his responsibility. That I'm the parent. I explain that I'm only sharing my experience with him, as a way of assuring him that his feelings are valid. *He isn't alone in this.* I both see him and understand.

We sat in that silence. Not quite together, but not apart either.

That night, Landon stays in his room. But he eats the strawberries I cut for breakfast. A quiet acceptance. A gesture that says, I'm not gone yet.

Fay has her own storm. She's painting a hot air balloon and it doesn't come out the way she wants. She wants to start over but I can't find a blank canvas, *even though I know we have a tote full of them somewhere.* She doesn't want to wait for the paint to dry to reuse the one she has. She wants a reset. Now. When she can't have it, she shuts everything down. Cleans up, slams her art bin closed and storms to her room. Screams into her air mattress and pillows. Hides under her blanket and growls when I check on her.

I give her space to feel her feelings *because in this moment she needs to.*

She comes out later and apologizes. Says she was frustrated at the situation, not me. She's sorry she took it out on me. I hug her tight. I tell her I understand *because I do.*

My husband spends the day working on job applications. Four private sector listings. One pays more than we've ever made. But it's in a place we don't want to go, and a job he doesn't want. Two are in New

Hampshire. One is remote. And they are all highly competitive. Even more now, with the job market flooded with displaced federal workers. He's qualified. He knows he is. He tells me, "This is something I can do."

He feels like he's on the edge of unraveling and trying to be proactive. He's hoping getting an offer will let us leave Florida or at the least negotiate an exit plan with his current job. Anything to get us unstuck.

At bedtime, I knock gently on Landon's door. He's lying on his bed, headphones in. "I'm going to give you a 20-second hug. Is that okay?" I ask him.

Years ago, I read about oxytocin hugs. How deep, sustained pressure can help regulate the nervous system. I started implementing this with the kids and my husband. It became our ritual. Even now, especially now.

He nods without saying anything out loud.
I wrap my arms around him. Firm and steady. And begin to count out loud.

"One, two, three..." I feel his shoulders slowly settle.

He lets me hold him.

I get to twenty, but I don't let go right away. *I never do.* I worry my count was too fast. I want to make sure it has time to work.

And maybe, if I'm honest with myself, I don't want to let go. Sometimes I think the tight hug is for me, too.

Eventually, I ease away. I kiss the top of his head and say our goodnights and leave the room for him to settle in for the night.

Fay is waiting for me with her tablet. It's our thing lately. Just the two of us, watching a show together while lying in her bed. A couple episodes a night. My husband is already asleep, knocked out from exhaustion by 7:30. I let him rest. I climb into Fay's bed, and we finish the series finale.

It's small, but it matters.
We sigh when it ends. "It was so good." she says. "But I'm sad it's over."

"Yeah…" I say. "We can find another show, but I liked this one."

It was witty. Emotionally intelligent. It gave us something, without taking too much. Something to share. Something to finish.

She turns off the tablet. I tuck her in. I brush the hair off her forehead and say, "I love you to the moon and back, around the world, a million times infinity, plus one."

She repeats it back.
I kiss her forehead and leave her room.

Then I sit in the hallway, alone. Letting it all settle.

Listening to the quiet. Hoping it holds. Because this is what motherhood looks like right now. Not always able to find a way to fix things. *Sometimes I'm not sure if I can even make anything better.* Just staying. Just loving them. Just trying again tomorrow.

Even when I don't know what comes next.

44.

Feel My Feelings

Today Fay and I had one of our talks. The kind where we sit in her bed and address and untangle the big feelings. I try to teach the kids how to release the pressure valve with internal reflection check-ins.

Sometimes Fay and I talk about topics that go deeper than most nine-year-olds have words for. But she's sharp. She's aware of the world around her just as much as the world inside herself. *Emotionally intelligent in ways I had to learn over years.* She's equipped with the skills I had to earn.

We talked about how we process the world, and I asked if I could read her something from my book that I'm writing. She listened. Nuzzled in close. Put her hand gently on my arm. When I finished, I asked what she thought.

She replied,
"Can I write something right now for your book?"
She asked me to type her words exactly as she said them.

What follows are her own words. Raw and unpolished:

"Hello my name is Fay. I'm the daughter of my mother and we have tragically lost our house in a flood. This isn't going to be very long. But I would just like to explain how I've been feeling. I feel like everything has changed a little too much for me. And I'm not really good with changes. Sometimes I feel very sad and I just need to cry.

But I mostly try to keep it in. I love our cat, but sometimes I think about what I will do when the cat sadly dies because he is getting older. I know that the cat is healthy for now, but I'm still scared I will lose my furry companion. Also, I love him so much, but sometimes he can be a little annoying. He wakes everyone up and I don't know what to do. But, what I know is, that big changes have happened and sometimes I just need to sit down and think. Sometimes I just need to face it and feel my feelings."

I never wanted my children to understand loss so young. I never wanted them to recognize the pattern of it. To worry about the next thing they could lose while still living in the last.

But in this house, we feel our feelings. We name them.

45.

Still Wild

It was an unusually dry day for April in Florida. I stood out in my yard and reflected on nature.

We used to visit the water often.

We'd kayak the river. The water was crystal clear and tricked your eyes when calm. It looks like you could reach down and touch the bottom with your fingertips, but it's actually well above your head if you were trying to stand. We would watch the manatees glide beneath us, their massive bodies visible through the deceptive clarity. We would point at the fish darting around the mangroves. Cheer, when Landon counted the mullet jumping.

Spontaneous and chaotic. As if the river had a sense of humor and wanted to share the joke with us.

Before school mornings, I'd bring Fay down to check for otters. Their sleek heads popping up like periscopes from under the dock, her small hand in mine as we scanned the surface. With my husband, I'd admire the calm. Those moments when the water turned to glass, reflecting sky so perfectly you couldn't tell where one ended and the other began. We'd explore hidden alcoves, secret pockets of river which felt like they belonged only to us, places you could only reach by water. By knowing where to look.

Now we watch the water from the dock. Still. Quiet. We don't paddle into it anymore.

The kayaks stay stacked under the overhang on the side of the house. Sometimes I catch myself looking at them. The paddles lean against the wall, collecting pollen and cobwebs that settle over things we've abandoned outside without meaning to.

It feels different when the water has visited your home uninvited.

When it has crawled up your walls.
And made a memory no amount of bleach could erase.

We haven't brought ourselves to get back in the kayaks. Not this time. Sometimes I get brave enough to dip my toes in the water, to feel that familiar coolness, but that's as far as courage takes me. It's not fear exactly, though fear lives there too, swimming just below the surface. It's a different kind of knowing. The river isn't a field trip anymore.

It's history.
It's a consequence.

It's mood, shifting and unpredictable as a teenager's temper.

This was supposed to be our dream. Living in a place like this, surrounded by nature. Waking up to river views and bird songs and falling asleep to the sounds of tree frogs echoing from the woods. We chose this house in the interest of its relationship with nature. Because we wanted to be close to something wild and beautiful. *But it was never meant to come into our home.*

The water that once felt like escape now feels like reckoning. Every time I look at it, I see it not just as it is, peaceful, reflecting clouds, home to herons and fish but as it was.

Rising.
Reaching.

Taking.

The kids still ask if we'll go out again someday, their voices carrying a particular hope that children master. *The kind that assumes broken things can always be fixed.* I nod since nodding feels easier than explaining. But I don't promise. Not because I'm scared of the water, but because I'm scared of how I might feel once I'm in it. If, I'll look back at the house from the water and feel that ache all over again. The one that sometimes lives in my chest like a second heartbeat.

If, I'll want to paddle until the river takes me somewhere else.
Somewhere that doesn't hold so much history.

Sometimes now, I daydream about escaping to a high-rise apartment, sealed away from it all. Climate-controlled. Predictable. Safe from the whims of weather and water. A place where nature stays outside where it belongs, framed in windows like art instead of living all around us with intentions.

But the truth is, I think a part of me will still miss this when we can finally leave. No matter where we end up. Even now, broken as my relationship with this place has become, I catch myself noticing the way morning light catches the Spanish moss. How a giant bird stands motionless in the shallows like a meditation on patience.

But we still try, in smaller ways, safer ways to stay connected. Learning to embrace and appreciate nature feels like an act of defiance now.

It doesn't come naturally as much as it used to.
But maybe that's what makes it matter more.

As part of homeschooling, we turn nature into curriculum, transforming our complicated relationship into lesson plans and field trips. We visit salt marshes and explore forests where the light filters through leaves like stained glass windows.

We identify trees by their leaves, oaks, maples, palms and pines. We point out native plants and animals. We learn bird calls by ear until the morning chorus becomes a familiar language. We talk about ecosystems and erosion. We examine how even the air changes when the canopy shifts, becoming cooler, and greener.

Thick with the exhale of growing things.

Sometimes we bring lesson plans and sometimes we don't. Sometimes it's enough just to go. To walk among things that grow without asking permission. Which bend without breaking. That know how to start over.

Some of the parks feel unchanged, frozen in the same beauty that drew us here in the first place. Others look beaten, wearing their markings openly. There are places where entire tree lines tilted in one direction, like they all tried to run from the same nightmare. Places where paths washed out and never came back, leaving scars in the earth that grass hasn't learned to cover yet.

We don't talk about that part much. The kids don't need another reminder of what can vanish overnight. *How quickly familiar becomes foreign.* But I see them noticing. I see the way their steps pause at a broken boardwalk, how their voices drop when we pass a tree split in half by wind.

My garden is overgrown now, swallowed by weeds growing faster than my motivation to fight them.

The vegetables, fruits and flowers, replaced by a jungle of green that grows wild and unplanned. I don't own a lawnmower anymore. It was another casualty, claimed by water and time and the particular exhaustion which comes from starting over too many times. But the neighbors take turns mowing the edges of my yard, their kindness delivered without expectation of fanfare.

When I can summon the energy, I go out with the manual lawn cutter, pacing back and forth over patches just to make walking paths through the green chaos. It's slow work, meditative in its repetition. The blade slices through stems with satisfying snaps, clearing space for my feet. *The possibility of control in small doses.* It's something. In a world where so much feels like too much.

It's something.

Sometimes I fantasize about planting again, about starting over with seeds and soil and the stubborn hope that makes gardens possible. I imagine neat rows and labels written on wooden stakes, the satisfaction of watching something grow because I willed it to. But I don't trust the soil anymore. I don't trust what will survive and what won't. The earth feels different now, like it's keeping secrets about what it might do next.

I don't want to replant roots here.
Not again

So I pull the biggest weeds when they offend me and leave the rest to their wild business. It's still green, I tell myself.

Wild green.
Chaotic green.
But green nonetheless.

That has to count for something.

Nature changed after both hurricanes. Last year's and this year's, each one teaching us new lessons about stubbornness or surrender.

There are more deer now, stepping delicately through our altered landscape and trotting down the weathered street like they're navigating a museum. There are more coyotes whose howls make the neighborhood dogs nervous. Wild turkeys strutting through the park like they own the place. *Which maybe they do now.*

Bobcats slip through our pathways. Raccoons and armadillos weave through the park and the yard with the confidence of things that have always belonged here more than we have. Hogs root through what used to be careful landscaping. Snakes sunbathe on the lawn where the children used to play. Bugs buzz and click and hum the songs of places returning to themselves.

The balance shifted, and so did we.

We're learning to live in a world where the boundary between inside and outside, tame and wild, planned and chaotic, has blurred.

***

Last year, in those first tender months after we started to rebuild, I found a chrysalis forming in my garden. A green pod dangling from one of the plants the flood hadn't taken. Swaying gently in the breeze like a small miracle. Every day I visited it, drawn by the promise it held. The kids joined me in tracking its progress. We read about migration and life cycles and host plants. And encouraged the chrysalis each day to keep growing.

It felt like we were building homes together, the caterpillar and I. Hope in its most literal form. Suspended from a branch, waiting for the right moment to become something else entirely.

Then one night we had a freeze, unseasonable and sudden, and the chrysalis died.

I didn't want to believe it at first. I kept checking for days, hoping for movement, for any sign that transformation was still possible. I'd stand in the garden in the early morning light. Coffee growing cold in my hands, willing that small green package to twitch, to split, to release the butterfly we'd all been waiting for. Instead it darkened and began to shrivel.

I didn't want the kids to see that lesson up close.
That some transformations don't finish.

That some don't survive the weather and hope sometimes dies in the cold despite our careful tending.

The plant where the chrysalis hung, didn't survive the second flood. But the butterflies still come, dancing through the weeds now. A colorful assortment of wings catching light as they navigate the chaos I've let grow. There might even be more than last year.

Sometimes I see the woodpeckers back at work on cedar trees by my fence. Their rhythmic hammering, a sound both destructive and creative. *Part of me wishes they would come closer.*

I want them to band together and pick a single tree.

Maybe that oak that leans a little too far toward the house, its roots loosened by the last storm. I fantasize about them weakening it just enough to drop it through the roof. Finish the job the hurricanes started. Get us out of this place where we love and hurt in equal measure. Where beauty and danger wear the same face.

There's always trees that lean a little too far, waiting for the right wind. Sometimes I catch myself looking up at them during thunderstorms, part dread and part hope tangled together like the Spanish moss.

Nature isn't comfort.
Not in the way it used to be.

But it's still moving. Still working its slow rebellion against our attempts to contain and control it. Still teaching us that we are smaller than we think, more fragile than we'd like to admit, more connected than we sometimes remember.

The river keeps flowing past our dock, carrying stories and sediment toward the Gulf. The kayaks are still patiently stacked waiting to be used again. And somewhere between the water that took and the water that gives, between the garden that was and the wilderness that is, we're learning to live with a love that's complicated.

A relationship with wildness that will never again be simple.

Perhaps, simple was never the point.
Maybe the point is learning to accept what can hurt us.
To tend to what might not survive.
To stay wild in a world that keeps trying to wash us clean.

Still wild in ways I'm only beginning to understand.
Still transforming in ways I'm learning to name.

46.

The Year the Balloons Were for Me

I woke up to the sound of quiet footsteps, bare feet on tile and the rustling of tissue paper. At first, I thought I was dreaming. But when I opened my eyes, it was still dark outside. 3 a.m. I lay there listening, too tired to move, but too curious to fall back asleep.

This is something we do for the kids. After they go to sleep the night before their birthdays, we decorate the house. Streamers, homemade signs, as many balloons as we can breathe air into and little surprises tucked in corners. So their first sight of the day is celebration. It's tradition. It's love. It's one of the ways we've tried to frame what birthdays can mean.

But this time... it was for me.

Our kids had woken up at 3 a.m. to decorate the house.

There were cards wrapped in layers of tape and wrapping paper. Drawings and a paper flower from Fay, *so intricate it took me a moment to realize it wasn't real.* She told me it was for the collection of flowers she's been making me for the last two years. The ones still sitting on my windowsill catching the light every morning. The ones which survived the storms.

They handed me a record player. Landon said it was his idea. "So you can listen to the music you love like you did when you were a teenager!" he said proudly. There were records too. Albums I had danced to in my bedroom, curled up with after heartbreaks and sung in the car loud enough to rattle windows. Music that had carried me through. And now it has carried me here. To this moment, surrounded by the people I love most. The ones who love me back in the most personal, beautiful ways.

My eyes started to well up and tears started streaming down my cheeks. They all looked alarmed. "What's wrong?" they asked, looking worried as if they upset me.

All I could say was, "I think this is the most thoughtful birthday I've ever had."

They wrapped their arms around me in a big group hug. Landon said, "You deserve to be celebrated."

And I did.
I do.

However, knowing that, finally really knowing that, brings up its own kind of grief. Because if this kind of care was possible, it always was.

Now I see how many years throughout my whole life I had spent pretending scraps were enough. Shrinking down my needs to fit other people's capacity. Trying to feel full on empty gestures.

I thought maybe I didn't like my birthday. But really, I just didn't like feeling invisible on a day that was supposed to mark my existence.

So yes, this birthday was beautiful.
But it was also complicated.

Because once you finally feel seen, you start to realize how long you've been invisible. How long you made yourself small enough to be overlooked.

This year, though, the house was covered in decorations hung with care. Someone remembered things I'd said in passing and turned them into gifts, instead of me having to pick my own.

There were no mind games like I remembered from when I was younger. No conditional acceptance like the kind I once thought was normal. No wondering if I was allowed to feel joy without a layer of guilt that someone had to go out of their way to make it happen.

The little girl inside of me, the one who had to prove she deserved celebration after the age of 10. The one who feared no one would even want to show up if there was a party. *She felt seen.*

There was music.
And laughter.
And hugs.

There were balloons and they were for me.

47.

Reverse Engineering the Stalemate

People keep asking why we don't just walk away. As if we haven't tried. As if we didn't already build the exit, only to watch it wash away.

I did everything I was supposed to do. Pictures taken. Lists written. Receipts gathered and sent. Questions answered. Additional explanations, given preemptively. Spreadsheets: filled in, cross-referenced, color-coded, filed, and attached. Re-sent when they mysteriously went "missing."

Every hoop they told me to jump through, I jumped. Higher. Faster. *More politely than I should have needed to.*

And still, still, the same reply. "We are working on it." "Be patient." But patience isn't what keeps me afloat anymore. *Patience is what drowns you when you stop kicking. I'm not patient. I'm trapped and there's a difference.*

"We appreciate your continued cooperation during this difficult time." Difficult time. I think about that phrase a lot. Difficult is when you lose a sock in the laundry and you have to fish it out from deep inside the vent. *This?* This is a slow hemorrhage of sanity.

I begged for updates. I followed up. I left polite nudges. I escalated quietly, seeing as loudness only gave them more reason to shuffle my name to the bottom of the stack.

When I got answers, they were vague. When I pressed for specifics, they ghosted me. No, not ghosted, that's too clean a word. They bled me out slowly through more waiting. Death by indifference.

So here I am, waiting again. Waiting on decisions that can't be made because this error-riddled "official report" is the gatekeeper to everything.

Repairs.
Loans.
Moving forward.
Breathing steadily again.

I reached out to lawyers, mortgage specialists, realtors, nonprofits and contractors. My insurance and my bank. No one had clear answers. Everyone suggested I ask someone else.

I tell myself, "You did what you were supposed to. This isn't your fault. You can only do so much." It helps a little but not enough to stop the old reflex. The one that whispers, *maybe you should have done more. Maybe you missed something.*

That's what living inside this system does.

It teaches you to doubt your own survival skills. It teaches you to sit still while your life is dismantled one administrative delay at a time.

I imagine yelling. I imagine sending emails written in fire. But I know better. I have learned to wield my rage like a scalpel, not a sledgehammer. One wrong move and they could punish me for not playing nice. So I smile through gritted teeth and draft another email that sounds like an apology for my own existence because survival isn't fair. *It's just what's necessary.*

When the claim report finally came in. I sat at the kitchen table, heart pounding, mind racing. The plastic sheeting still clung to the exposed studs of the walls around me, a half-gutted house breathing humidity into the room. I opened the file. Skimmed line after line. I could see it immediately, it appeared to be partially copy-pasted from the year before.

There were missing items, lowball estimates, inconsistencies everywhere representing an old floorplan and appliances we had no longer owned or had replaced. He hadn't let me review it. Hadn't called, hadn't checked in. Just filed it without warning. And now this botched report was the current official record of our loss.

I immediately called the insurance carrier before I even finished reading. I listed the mistakes out loud. Advised them not to approve the report until it was fixed. They told me to email the details. I did. I reached out to the adjuster too.

No one at the insurance company replied even though they requested I put it in writing and send it to them.

My adjuster seemed offended. He told me he had read every single one of my emails and texts at least ten times. *From my perspective, that obviously wasn't true.* And when I pointed out the information he missed and showed him the proof that it was sent, he told me I was getting caught up on the details. As if I should be congratulating him for his "hard work."

But I wasn't about to thank someone for documenting our devastation wrong.

Waiting had gotten me nowhere. So I stopped. I opened my laptop. Looked up our adjuster by name and the details I knew about him. I found his license, his credentials, the software he used. *It wasn't hard.*

If he won't cooperate with me, I'll just have to teach myself how to do his job instead. I downloaded everything I could find. Policy guides, claim manuals, report templates, samples, and glossaries. Reverse engineering the stalemate.

Maybe I can't break the system open. Maybe I can't change the rules. But I can learn them. And I can find every crack they tried to pretend wasn't there.

***

If I really said what I was thinking, I know people would get hung up on the idea of defiant anger, *but I've never been quite comfortable with anger*. It wasn't like I was looking for a reason to feel betrayed. To feel my blood boil beneath my skin at some kind of interpreted injustice.

People ask, "What radicalized you?"

As if it's a moment. A protest. A book. A dramatic shift from tame to furious.

But I was never radicalized.
I was raised in the rot.

There was no sudden awakening, just a slow accumulation of evidence I wasn't allowed to ignore. Maybe it's the autism, the pattern-seeking, the refusal to let polite fiction overwrite observable reality. Maybe it's just being born into a generation where contradiction is the baseline.

I saw racism before I could truly identify it. I watched how people's eyes changed when they looked at my mother in public. I didn't even fully understand that I was biracial, just that something in me made people recalibrate. Teachers. My peers. Cashiers. Neighbors.

It was all there.
And no one called it what it was.

I watched the Twin Towers collapse after descending the steps of a middle school bus and didn't understand yet that I was about to live in the shadow of that collapse for decades. Through war, divisive debates of how to protect our nation while preserving our values, and an economy that would keep shedding its stability like snake skin.

I watched my dad, a business owner, come home quiet after layoffs. He didn't say much but I knew what it meant. Someone's rent wouldn't be paid. Someone's kids would pay the price. People he cared about, would go without and there was nothing that he could do to fix it.

Someone else was carrying the cost of a system none of us could control.

I played by the rules. Took jobs that didn't pay enough to live on, so I compensated by working multiple jobs at one time. *I still got told to feel lucky.* Then I got the degree, just to graduate into a recession. Homeownership wasn't a rite of passage for most of us without help from family. It became a feat of survival and for those of us who managed to get there, it was often temporary.

I was a homeowner.
Then I lost everything.
Then it happened again.

The insurance we paid heavily for didn't come to save us. Bureaucracy didn't bring relief.

I've met other flood survivors across the political spectrum who see the same cracks in the system. Some of us might disagree on solutions but we all know something's broken when working families can't rebuild after disasters.

We all want to keep our children safe.
For our work and effort to matter.
And for our communities to thrive.

We are told to lift ourselves up by our bootstraps. To adapt. To build resilience. But I want to tell you something about bootstraps: they're slippery when they're wet. *And it feels like I've been trudging through mud for years.* My feet heavy with debt, loss, and the weight of things I'm still not allowed to grieve fully because someone else had it worse.

Above us are bridges. Clean, dry bridges. Held up by trust funds and tax shelters. And the people on those bridges look down at us, the ones wading through floodwaters, bills, and emptying savings. Dwindling resources and options. And ask why we're not walking faster. Why, we look so bitter? Why we're not smiling more.

They call us radical for noticing the imbalance.

But we're not radical.
We're exhausted.

We are the people that did everything we were told to do in a crumbling house with a rigged foundation. Yet we still got blamed when it collapsed. Like holding it up with our own hands, would have ever been enough to keep something standing that was designed to fall apart.

We don't want to burn it all down.
We just want to stop being the kindling.

I'm not angry because I expected more. I'm angry because I wanted to believe them. I craved peace and tried to do what was asked of me, hoping I wasn't being strung along.

I just wanted everything to work the way it should.

But it doesn't.

So I stopped waiting. I study. I trace their footprints. I write their acronyms and limits on sticky notes. I learn the rules they thought I wouldn't find. I build a file they can't ignore. As long as I'm going to be held hostage by paperwork, then I'll turn it into a blueprint.

If I'm going to be punished for asking questions, then I'll become the expert they didn't see coming.

48.

A Couch in a Room Without Walls

Today is our fourteenth wedding anniversary. Instead of going out or making grand plans, we decided to buy a couch.

The couch is nothing fancy. It arrived compressed inside a single cardboard box. Small enough to make Greg and I glance at each other in silent question:

"Is that really going to fit us?"

The box looked too small for what we needed. Too small for what we hoped it could be.

We tear it open and nothing moves. Everything is still tightly packed. Modular parts, green corduroy cushions vacuum-sealed flat and brackets loose yet barely shifting in their bag. It was as if we were playing Tetris in reverse, every shape needing to be pulled apart instead of pushed together.

There were more pieces than we expected.
More steps.
More work.

But all four of us pitched in. Fay took charge of the cushions. Carrying them carefully into her room so they wouldn't get dirty on the floor. Landon crouched next to Greg, steadying the frame while we tapped the brackets into place. I knelt on the rug, fitting parts together, the motion already familiar from a thousand other rebuilds.

With each click of a bracket, each stretch of fabric pulled tight, the couch started to grow larger than the box had suggested.

It started to become real.
By the time we finished,
it was unmistakably a couch.

We slid the area rug into place. Positioned the couch frame in its new home. We pulled one of the gifted side tables we got from our neighbor, next to the arm rest. We stood back to admire our work. The four of us lined up like judges at a small-town competition. I laughed. "It looks like a real living room." I said. "If you pretend we have drywall."

And in a way, it did.
In a way, it was.

We had built a little floating island of normalcy. A small, imperfect escape anchored inside an unfinished world.

We all gathered in front of it, grinning.

"Three, two, one." And we all sat down at once. Fay threw her arms up and exclaimed, "We all fit!" Her voice rang through the hollow space, full of a kind of wonder only children know how to claim without apology.

The couch isn't deep. It's not plush. It's not a couch you could buy from a furniture store that has a showroom. It's a little awkward, honestly. It's the kind of couch where you sink in just far enough that you lose head support and have to hold yourself upright. It's not the kind of couch we would have chosen before.

But it's ours.
It's real.

It's enough.

We decide to leave one of the hammocks up in the corner. Not because we have to anymore but because we want to. Because the idea of swinging gently beside a couch feels more like a choice now, and less like a desperate accommodation forced by the missing pieces of our home.

It's a small thing.

But it feels big.
It feels like a reclamation.

We have a couch. We have a living room. Not because the walls are finished, or because the house is whole, but because we decided to build something cozy in the middle of the wreckage anyway.

Because sometimes you don't wait for the world to fix itself around you.

Sometimes you claim the softness anyway. Even if you have to build it from a box too small and a room still broken, in a home that is supposed to be temporary.

Even if you have to hold your own head up.

49.

The Architecture of After

It's mornings like this, when my eyelids barely hold themselves open. When every breath is something I have to remember to take. When I sip from a coffee mug I've reheated too many times to count and still can't seem to finish. The house is quiet. Almost peaceful, but my chest is already tight. I wake up feeling stuck. I wake up feeling trapped.

It's not a new feeling. But it always pretends to be.

I press my tongue to the roof of my mouth and breathe in slowly.

One. Two. Three. Four.

Hold.
Exhale.

One. Two. Three. Four.

I try to ground myself.
Relax your tongue.
Stop clenching your jaw.
Breathe again.

What do I hear?
The birds chirp outside the window. The refrigerator hums. The fan clicks as it spins. My stomach grumbles.

What do I smell?
I smell coffee. I smell the onions I forgot to throw out, sitting stale in the kitchen.

Already behind.
Why didn't I clean that up last night?

Stop.

One. Two. Three. Four.

What do I taste?
I taste too much creamer in my diluted coffee.

What do I feel?
I feel the corduroy of the couch under my arms. The fibers of the rug between my toes. The breeze that barely makes it to this side of the room.

What do I see?
I see the blue tassels on the hammock beside me. My cat stretched out at the other end of the couch. Boxes still stacked. Rust-stained tile I can never get clean. A broom with its bristles halfway escaped from the handle.

It feels like there is a vice grip around my forehead. It's going to force my skull to cave in.

The non-existent walls are closing in. The room is beginning to spin again.

I want to escape too.

But out of what?
It's different this time.

Stop.

Why won't they let me leave?
I said please.
Please don't...

STOP! This isn't the same.

One. Two. Three. Four.

Time starts to reverse. It speeds up. Then it melts away. My eyes continue to frantically dart back and forth. My body is frozen like someone is holding me down.

I'm not nineteen anymore. I'm not floating outside my body under the weight of that man twice my size.

I'm not helpless.
I know that now.

One. Two. Three. Four.

But I also know what surrender looks like.
What it costs.
What it steals that never fully comes back.

I thought if I just got out, I could move on. I know better now. And I keep pushing forward, even when I don't want to. Because I know what stopping means. I know what it feels like to vanish from yourself. To live years trying to crawl back to something no one else can see is missing.

I don't want my children to learn that kind of silence.
I don't want them to ever become familiar with its ache.

I am still imprisoned.

How can this keep happening?

I may not be trapped in a room. There may be no lock on the door. But I am trapped again. *Just in a different way.* This is still my life. Still my future.

And I refuse to let anyone or any system... take that from me. *Not again.*

One. Two. Three. Four.

Sometimes I imagine my brain is like a house after a hurricane. It has been gutted and restructured by someone other than me. Wired back together by someone in a hurry. Someone who didn't label anything and left the job half-done.

Some of the light switches still work. Others don't. Some flip on the wrong fixtures. A hallway fan when I meant to light the kitchen. An outdoor floodlight, instead of the soft lamp I used to read beside. A few hum quietly, even when they're off. *Like a warning of something about to spark.*

There are places I've learned not to touch.

The attic crawlspace of certain memories. The closet where I store what I don't want to face. The back hallway that echoes too loudly with footsteps that aren't there anymore.

It's not just the wiring that's faulty. It's the whole blueprint that has been rearranged without my consent. Rooms where there used to be open space. Walls where there used to be doors. I keep trying to navigate it like it's still the old layout. I keep bumping into things that used to comfort me. I flip the switch I think will turn on calm, but instead, it floods the room with anxiety. Or shame. Or nothing at all.

Hypervigilance isn't just being on edge. It's living in a house where you don't know which breaker is about to blow. It's waiting for the power to fail. *It's hearing the low but constant electric buzzing and wondering if you're the only one who hears it.*

Trauma lives in the walls now.

In the hum. In the static.
I can't always see it.
But I know it's there.

I never know what will trip the system next.

Here's the shift I'm still working on.

Slowly.
Painfully.

Resilience isn't about proving I can endure everything. It's not about showing the world how much I can carry without breaking. It's about learning when to put things down, even temporarily. It's about choosing rest, softness, and presence so I can continue on. It's about finding steadiness in the middle of chaos, instead of building higher walls around myself every time the wind picks up. It's about building something better inside myself.

Not because I owe it to anyone.

But because I want to live.
Really live.

Healing isn't linear. It isn't clean. It doesn't erase what happened. It doesn't promise you'll never bleed through your stitches again. *Even if it's not what I hoped for, maybe that's okay.* Maybe just plain surviving isn't the goal anymore. Maybe surviving was just the first step and now the work is learning how to live.

After all this time *and despite my protests*, the truest thing I know is this:

I didn't survive because I was stronger than the storm. I survived because I showed up anyway. Even when it hurt. Even when it felt impossible. Even when I didn't recognize the person staring back at me in the mirror.

And maybe that's enough.

Maybe the quiet moments, the ones without proving, without bracing, the ones where I simply breathe, simply exist, are the ones that mean I'm still winning.

Not against trauma.
Not against pain.

Not for the sake of being labeled resilient.

But for myself.
And for today, for right now, I'll cling to that.

One. Two. Three. Four

50.

Coffee and Change

Soft or Hardened?

In therapy this week, my therapist was talking about how pressure and hardship, like boiling water, can change things.

She referenced the way boiling water softens vegetables but hardens an egg. Both are transformed by the same force. Yet each responds in its own way. It's a striking image, but as I listened, I found myself wrestling with it.

I don't want the world to harden me.

I've spent so much of my life building kindness, vulnerability, and open-heartedness. *These are the qualities I treasure in myself.* They're the reasons I've been able to do the work that I do. To connect with people who have been through the worst, to see them, and help them see themselves. *The thought of becoming cold or rigid in response to the world's pressures terrifies me.* It's as if, deep down, I believe that softness is my strength. The one thing I can rely on to keep moving through the world. *No matter how difficult it gets.*

But then, something in me shifted as I thought more about her words. I considered the egg.

Boiling water hardens the egg, yes, but it also makes it safe to eat. It transforms something fragile into something durable. And without that change, the egg could potentially be dangerous to consume. Without that heat, the egg remains raw, vulnerable to bacteria, and could result in illness.

The world can feel like boiling water at times.

It's often unforgiving. Painful. Testing my limits. But in its pressure, it forces something inside of me to harden.

So what's the truth?
Should I fear hardening?
Or should I embrace it?

Maybe, just maybe, I can allow both. Maybe the world can change me, but that doesn't mean I have to lose myself in the process. It's not about becoming hardened to everything. But rather hardening in the areas where I need protection and growth. All while keeping the parts of me I can still soften in the right moments.

I continued to think of the work I've done in advocacy. Speaking for, and with, those who've had their voices shushed. Organizing groups. Fighting for change.

I think of the vulnerability required to step into those spaces, to share my story when it would be easier to stay hidden. And I realize that maybe the world is right in a sense. It does change us.

The balance, I think, is in choosing where and when I harden and where I allow myself to soften. I want to remain soft in my compassion, my empathy, and my ability to understand. But I also need to know when to harden just enough to keep moving forward. Even when I feel exposed. Even when the world feels too much to bear.

As I struggled with these ideas, my therapist said "I think instead of boiling eggs or vegetables, you are making coffee."

"What if it's all part of the same transformation?"

With coffee, it's the water that transforms the grounds into something new. It's not a sudden change. It's gradual. Over time, it shifts. The bitter becomes richer, the process more refined. Perhaps the pressure, the boiling water, doesn't destroy, it refines us. Molds us into something stronger. Yet more aware of our fragility.

I don't have all the answers. I think that's what makes this process of transformation beautiful and terrifying. It's not about being an egg or a vegetable, soft or hard, vulnerable or invincible. It's about finding a way to exist in the space between it all. To allow for both softness and strength in a world that asks us to be one or the other. Both adaptions are valid.

So maybe I'm not just making coffee.
But becoming coffee.
A little bit of both.

I Am Coffee:

I depend on coffee.
It's a part of my rhythm,
my daily ritual.

It wakes me up,
gives me a boost.
A reason to keep going.

I am often the one who fuels me through the day.
The steady companion in the morning fog.
The jolt to my system.

But what if, in some strange way,
I am someone's coffee?

Not in the way I thought before,
where I'm supposed to be a source of grand inspiration.
Pushing people toward greatness,
becoming a catalyst for change.

Maybe it's not about inspiring after all.
Maybe it's about simply being there.
Quiet, comforting, steady.

Like that warm mug in hand on a Sunday morning.
When the world hasn't yet woken up.

Coffee isn't for everyone.
Some people disdain it.
Can't stand the taste.
The way it lingers on their tongue.
The way it sometimes leaves them jittery.

They prefer tea instead.

A gentler ritual.
A quieter energy.
And that's okay.

I don't need to be for everyone.
I don't need to be anyone's lifeline.
I don't need to be enough for anyone.
Not even for myself.

There's a time and place for everything.

For coffee, for tea, for quiet moments.
For the loudness of life.
For growth, for rest.

And even after the coffee is made,

even after it's consumed,
I don't discard the grinds.

I keep them,
because they still have purpose.

They can help my garden grow.
Nourish what comes next.
I don't throw away what's left of me.

In the end,
I am more than the cup I'm poured into.

I am also what I leave behind.
What I give without even trying.

I am the warmth.
The comfort.
The possibility of a new day.

51.

Crumbs Between Alarms

Lately, I've noticed something I don't quite know how to explain.

The world hasn't calmed down, but somehow, I have. It's not that the stress has disappeared. My life is still built on missing drywall, flood stained floors, government delays, and every what-if that comes with disaster recovery. Yet somehow, the chaos isn't clanging in my head the way it used to.

I still get overwhelmed. I still cry in short, exhausted bursts. But the tightness in my chest that once felt permanent, like an alarm I couldn't reach to silence, has gone quiet. Not gone. Just... no longer screaming.

And it feels strange.

For most of my life, I operated from a kind of internal readiness. Like a soldier who never fully takes off their boots. Always waiting for the next emotional ambush, the next betrayal, the next shift in tone that would confirm I was being misunderstood again. That was my normal.

Now that the pulse of hypervigilance has slowed, part of me keeps asking, *am I missing something? Shouldn't I be on edge? If the world still isn't safe, why do I feel more steady?*

I think the answer is this. My nervous system isn't confusing quiet with danger in the same way it used to. *I'm not bracing for impact every time I exhale.* It's not disassociation. I know what that feels like.

The numb float, the glaze of survival over my skin.

This is different. I feel present. I feel plugged into my body. In tune with my children, my husband and myself.

Maybe this is what happens when you stop needing everyone else to tell you who you are. When you stop chasing clarity from people who only offer distortion. When you start believing your inner compass over the external noise.

The absence of panic isn't emptiness.
It's space.
It's capacity.

I haven't reached this sense of peace because life got easier. I reached it because I stopped abandoning myself in the middle of the storm.

But this peace doesn't fully erase anger. *Peace doesn't have to mean you've made peace with everything that's happened.*

I stood in the kitchen staring at the toaster tray. It was overflowing with crumbs, burnt, curled, charred edges of bread we'd forced through the machine for weeks. I hadn't cleaned it. *I don't know why that was the moment that cracked me open. But it was.*

I tapped the tray into the trash, watched the crumbs scatter and I thought, *maybe this is what survival has turned into.* Managing debris. Rearranging waste. Pretending that effort and endurance are the same as living.

I've been collecting crumbs in every corner of my life. Not just food. Not just in this kitchen. I mean the way I've been spoken to. The way people check in just enough to keep the relationship technically alive. The way systems say "we care!" but then close the case. The way I've told myself any progress counts, even when it's a standstill with better lighting.

They call you strong for enduring. They don't ask how much you've lost in the process. You get compliments instead of help. Funding offers instead of real support. "Let us know if you need anything." But you've already learned not to ask.

Crumbs. All of it. Crumbs.

I keep saying thank you because I'm not allowed to be angry without being seen as ungrateful. Let's be honest, if I raise my voice, they'll say I'm hysterical. If I tell the truth, they'll mark my file as difficult and move on.

So I scrape the crumbs into the bin and try again. Apply again. Explain again. Perform resilience again. Smile again.

And all of it still feels like not enough.

Not enough help. Not enough healing. Not enough of me left to keep going like this.

There's nothing romantic about barely holding it together. Nothing noble about patching a life back together out of salvaged parts. No glory in learning how to ask less and accept less, just to keep the peace.

But there is clarity and that clarity has taken root in the quiet.

I want to be done being grateful for crumbs. I want to be angry without being punished. I want to be seen without having to bleed first. I want to be heard before it becomes a story someone else tells for credit.

And I want that now.

Not when I've earned it.
Not when the crisis is over.
Not when it's convenient to applaud my "grace under pressure."

Now.

Surviving isn't the same as being okay and crumbs are not a meal.

Maybe I'm not healing in a way that's loud or triumphant. Maybe I'm just finally living in the space between alarms.

52.

The Quiet Yes

It starts before I even notice. The subtle slip of my thoughts.

The way I open the document, but don't type.
The way my body curls in, small without meaning to.
The way my breathing thins out, barely audible.

Not thinking productively yet.
Just gone.
I stare at the cursor blinking on the empty page.
The flood rushes up, no warning.

Don't tell them. Don't hurt them. Don't make it real!

My hands begin to tremble.
I set them flat on my thighs like it will anchor me, but it doesn't.

The old dread presses tight against my chest.
You're selfish. You're dramatic. You're wrong.

Their voices, their words...
No, my voice now, too.

It's happening again.
The invisible shrinking.

The internal negotiations have started before I can put a stop to them.

Maybe if I write it differently.
Maybe if I leave that part out.
Maybe if I make myself smaller, more restrained, easier to love.

Maybe, maybe, maybe!

I close my eyes.
Inside my head, there is no lasting peace.
It's a battlefield.

Fragments firing off everywhere.

You're lucky it wasn't worse.
You should be grateful.
You're exaggerating.
Other people had it harder.

The noise is unbearable.
The ache behind my eyes is sharp.

I almost close the laptop.
I almost walk away from myself.
I almost choose it again.

The disappearing.

But then,
quietly, stubbornly,
another voice.

Smaller than the others. But heavier somehow and real.

Remember you don't owe them your disappearance anymore.
A reminder I keep needing.

It's not a shout.

It's barely a whisper.

But it hits like a bell ringing inside my own consciousness. I press my palms into the laptop, trying to ground myself again. I feel the shake in my arms, the sting behind my eyes.

I let it be there.
I let it all come.

The fear.
The grief.
The guilt I was taught to carry as part of myself.

It doesn't drown me.
It doesn't kill me.
I let it move its way through me.

Maybe the truth is not the violence. Maybe the hiding was.

I open my eyes.
The cursor still blinks.
It's waiting for me.

No judgment.
No punishment.
Just ready.

I type the first sentence.

It feels wrong.
It feels right.

I keep going.

Not because it's safe.
Not because it's easy.

But because trying to stay true to myself is something I haven't fully abandoned yet.

The morning light shifts across the floor.
Soft. Golden. Indifferent.

The story tilts.

...I'm writing a book.

53.

Exit Wounds

I sit back. The glow of the monitor hums against my skin.

The report, my supplemental insurance report, is really pulling together. Built from the ground up with my hands. *But now what?*

There's a fork here, a hesitation sharp enough to taste.

Technically, I can submit it myself. I've read the regulations. Memorized the deadlines. Legally, nothing says I have to keep waiting on him. But legally isn't the same thing as practicality.

I know how this game is played. I know the silent rules. The ones not written in the policy, but etched into every email delay and ignored voicemail. If I go around him, the insurance company might ignore me. Pretend they never got it. Or worse, punish me for stepping out of line. If I send it to the adjuster, maybe he'll submit it under his name.

Maybe he'll tweak it just enough to call it his own and he'll get paid for my work. Or maybe he doesn't want to bring any attention to his mistakes. *What would that look like?*

A bitter taste rises in my throat. I don't want him to touch it. But I want, *no, need,* the claim to move forward.

What matters more, credit or closure?

I run the calculations in my head.
Pros. Cons. Outcomes.

No best option.
No choice pure.

***

I pull out a notebook and start listing strategies:

1. Send it directly to the insurance desk. I risk being ignored but I have documentation of my effort.

2. Send it to the adjuster. Maybe more effective, but I would feel the sting of surrendering my work.

3. Do both, submit to the adjuster, CC the claim handler, timestamp everything.

Manage what I can, and keep documenting everything else. I sit with it. Not rushing, not reacting, just... considering.

A flicker of something steadier builds inside me. This isn't about him anymore or even about just the money. This is about showing up for myself again. About not abandoning my own work just because someone else might. About not folding because the system is designed to make me tired enough to quit.

I didn't realize how much I'd been holding onto until the moment I let it go.

Not the house, not the things, though I'd been gripping those too, but the belief that I could still somehow make the system work if I just documented hard enough. If I just revised the language. If I just named the grout width, the wall texture, the brand of the fridge again. If I chased the missing lines like a lawyer building a case for a crime everyone pretended didn't happen the way we remembered.

I was told giving up meant possible bankruptcy or foreclosure that could affect my husband's career. The other option was getting stuck here rebuilding again just in time for another hurricane season to possibly take it all again. We were told it meant giving up our hopes of a stable future. I thought giving up would feel like failure.

But they were wrong.
So I was wrong.

It felt like relief.

I was done trying to get someone to see what 28 inches of brackish water does to a kitchen when it seeps behind cabinets and lifts butcher block counters out of place like loose teeth. Done asking for validation through footage measurements and line items that no one seemed interested in adding unless I made it impossible for them not to.

I had rewritten the missed item list over and over. Each draft tighter and more legible. Each version carefully separating emotion from evidence, as if trauma belonged in a footnote. I had held my breath every time I emailed it, thinking maybe this was the time I'd hear back with something other than delay or dismissal.

But there was little to no reply. *There never was, not of substance at least.* Just the low-level hum of waiting as days went by and our lives stayed paused. Still living in a house with missing walls, pretending the exposed studs were a design choice.

It's strange how the moment of clarity didn't come with drama. No slamming laptops or rage-typed messages. It came on a quiet afternoon when I was rereading my own notes trying to finalize my insurance supplemental and I realized something. *I don't want to fix this anymore.*

I don't want to rewrite this file. I don't want to do their job for them, in hopes that they might take me seriously. And maybe throw me a few thousand more dollars, so I can maybe feel slightly less robbed.

I wanted to stop negotiating for scraps.

So I did.

I closed the file, not with defeat, but with finality. The kind that comes after too many second chances. I stopped writing the supplemental. Stopped chasing what was never going to be enough. And in that quiet refusal, I made space for something louder.

I don't know if that moment was my second wind or a death rattle.

Maybe it wasn't clarity.

Maybe it was just the sound I made before they flattened me for good. Maybe, I wasn't coming back to life. Maybe, I was just tired enough to stop pretending I ever would.

But I kept going anyway. We're leaving on our terms. We refuse to let anyone back us into repairing what's broken. We're not trying again. We're not asking them to see us anymore. We are tearing this page out of the book and writing our own ending.

***

That night, I laid it all out. Literally.

The bed was covered in papers, printed letters, appeals, county flood-plain policies, ICC eligibility criteria, scribbled notes and numbers that probably only made sense to me.

Every page had highlighter slashes in five colors, margin notes, drawn arrows and circles. My computer was open with 16 tabs. Employee relocation policy, FEMA's handbook, flood zone elevation calculators, real estate comps for flood lots, contractor quotes, and county building department resource guides.

It looked like a crime board. Red yarn in my brain, sticky notes cross-referenced, contingency paths sketched like attack maps. A manifesto in bullet points, some circled so hard I tore the page.

My husband walked into the bedroom while I was mid-sprawl, sitting cross-legged on the air mattress, in the middle of the chaos like a spider in her web. I didn't look up. I just started talking.

"This is the plan…" I said.

I told him we were going to file for Substantial Damage. That we'd make them admit that it shouldn't be repaired.

Insurance says they will only pay for repairs that will bring the structure back to its pre-flooded condition. Before Helene, our house could still legally be repaired.

I want to be paid what it would cost to have a legally repairable house again!

I told him that we'd use the designation to unlock the full $250,000 policy limit so we could pay off the majority of our mortgage. That we'd initiate the increased cost of compliance (ICC) coverage claim, which could be up to $30,000 before we ever handed over the property deed to anyone. That we'd force their hand and walk away free.

No more rebuilding. No more fighting for scraps. No more trying to earn what we'd already paid for.

I was talking a mile a minute.

My mouth could barely keep up with my mind. The contingencies, the parallel tracks, the "if-this-then-that" logic trees I'd built like a spreadsheet with formula cells in my head. I didn't stop to breathe fully. I just kept going. I regurgitated weeks of strategy like a lifeline made out of paperwork and bold print.

And he just listened.

At first, his face was tight. Eyes darting over the papers like he wasn't sure what to make of the mess. I could see the gears grinding. Too much. Too fast. Too layered. I braced myself for the sigh. For the shutdown.

But then something shifted. He smirked. That half-smile he makes when he knows I've figured something out that no one else could see. When he stops feeling helpless and starts feeling like he's on a team that might actually win.

He looked at me, not just with relief, not just with admiration, but with pride. "You've figured it out!" he said. "You really figured it out!" And then "Yes. Do it!"

No hesitation.
No caveats.
Just yes.

It was the first time in months that "yes" felt like momentum.

We weren't stuck anymore. We weren't frozen, waiting on someone else to decide what we were allowed to do. We were moving. *And this time, it was our move.*

This isn't giving up.

It's calling it what it is.
And choosing not to live like that anymore.

***

The next morning, I woke up early, before the kids were stirring. My browser tabs were still alive like watchful eyes. The sun was bleeding through crooked hanging window blinds like it was trying to make its way into a space it didn't recognize anymore.

I barely finished my first cup of coffee. I didn't shower. I just sat down wrapped in my robe, barefoot on the cold grimy tile and opened a blank email.

It was the first time in over a year that I wrote to an official contact, without apology in my tone. No justification for the ask. Just facts. The waterline. The insurance estimate. The exposure to flood risk that was now historical, *not hypothetical*. I didn't ask for permission. I stated our position.

It was my belief the house was no longer viable. We are requesting official documentation that confirms what we already know.

We're done pretending this is salvageable for us.

I triple-checked the attachments and hit send before I could second-guess myself. Then I opened a new tab. My claim folder. The email to my adjuster.

This one took longer. Not that I didn't know what I wanted to say, but because I wanted it to be clean. No thread of negotiation. Just closure and direction.

I told him we were pivoting. I thanked him for his time, *even if the lack of cooperative communication had said more than the correspondence*. I let him know we'd be in touch once we had the official letter in hand. *And I meant it.*

The send button didn't feel like a gamble this time. It felt like a hammer drop. Not a hope but a claim. A claim to leave. *A claim to close.*

I stood up, closed the lid of the laptop, and started folding an empty box.

54.

The Email That Moved the House

Our insurance adjuster had replied within hours of the email I sent him. Just a short message.

"Understood. Good luck with the ICC."

It wasn't warm. It wasn't really encouraging. But it was a response. Which after months of communication that felt like pulling teeth and his most recent ghosting of my sent corrections, felt like a miracle. Still, I couldn't sit idle. My brain wouldn't let me trust it was enough.

I still ruminated on the email I had concurrently sent to my county's floodplain division. I wrote it carefully, attached all the documentation, and tried to make it clear that I wasn't just asking for a favor. I was following the rules, playing their game, using the right language.

I kept spiraling, refreshing my inbox. *What if I sent it to the wrong address? What if no one read it? What if it sits unread in some digital inbox purgatory for weeks like everything else had?*

So less than 24 hours later, I followed up. I pulled up an old email thread from last fall. One I had sent just after the hurricane, the one asking about picking up the debris. I reached out directly to the county official I had spoken to back then. I didn't expect a reply. Not quickly, anyway. Certainly not before the end of the day.

But I got one.

And that reply? It changed everything.

They confirmed it. Substantial damage was estimated. In writing. From the county. An actual letter on letterhead, with calculations and thresholds. A letter that finally makes other people listen. That makes insurers pay attention. That makes things real.

I could feel it in my body before I could put it into words. This was the first solid traction we'd gotten in over seven months.

My heart started racing. Not fear-racing, but the racing that happens when something breaks loose from under you and you're not falling, you're accelerating. My stomach flipped. My legs felt like jelly. I was halfway between screaming and sobbing and couldn't do either, so I bolted.

I ran into the living room and my daughter turned to me with wide eyes. *Alarmed.*

"What's wrong?" she asked.

"Good news," I managed to choke out. I was vibrating. My hands were shaking. "I need to tell Dad. He's on a call."

I tried to wait. I really did.

She watched me. *Nine years old and already too familiar with what it looks like when your mom is trying not to come apart.* But then she tilted her head and asked, "What is it?" I paused. *Could she understand what this meant? But she already did.*

We'd told her the plan. Told her about the long game. About the county and the letters and the insurance. She knew. And she put it together faster than I expected. Her eyes lit up like a fire had been sparked behind them.

Her mouth dropped open. "Wait, this is *the* letter?"
I nodded.

She screamed. "YES! Should we dance?"
We did.

We danced through the living room and the unfinished hallway, the floor still raw and weathered. Her socks slipping on the tile and my feet sliding on joy. We whooped and spun and jumped like the house couldn't hold us anymore. Like it wasn't ours, *or wouldn't be for long.*

She shouted, "Let's go tell Landon!"

We burst into his room like we were announcing a victory. I gave him the rundown. His face stayed still for a second. Processing. Like he was giving himself permission to believe it. Then he grinned.

"Nice," he said. "You're doing it."

I didn't realize until then that they'd been holding their breath too.

We heard my husband's footsteps in the living room. His call was over. "What's going on?" he asked, stepping in. I couldn't stand anymore after running back into the living room. I collapsed onto the couch, *the one we'd just assembled a few days before. The one that made the room feel almost like a home. Even though we had no drywall and slept on air mattresses.* I looked at him and told him.

"I got the email. The county confirmed it! It's most likely substantial damage! We're moving forward!" His shoulders dropped. Then tensed. Then dropped again. I watched his body try to remember how to feel hope. He sat down beside me and stared at the screen.

We both did.

And then, there it was. That flicker of light strengthening in his eyes.

The one that used to live there before the storms, before the waiting, before everything we built was soaked and stripped down to studs.

We looked at each other like people crawling out of a tunnel who just saw the sky. We started saying it out loud. To each other. Over and over like we needed to make it real.

"This is it."

"We're doing it."
"We're getting out."

We all jumped in the living room. The whole family. Four bodies in motion, grief ungluing itself from our legs just long enough to bounce. Right there in front of that new green couch, in a house we were about to say goodbye to.

It's not over. *We know that.* There's still paperwork and timelines and logistics and things that can go wrong. But for the first time in over a year, we aren't stuck. We are moving. And that, in itself, is a kind of closure. Not the final page, but maybe finally, the next chapter.

The kids wandered back to their rooms, laughing and light. The air in the house shifted, thinner somehow, like we'd just opened all the windows even though none of them budged. And then it was just the two of us.

No words for a moment. Just a long, tight hug. The kind that speaks in breath and pressure. That says I know what this cost and I see what you carried. I felt his chest rise, then fall, then stay still.

"Thank you," he whispered into my shoulder, his voice raw but steady. "Thank you for getting us out of this mess."

I squeezed tighter. Not out of effort, but out of relief.
Tears pricked at my eyes.

But this time, they were the right kind.

Happy tears.
Finally.

55.

Whiplash

The relief lasted exactly eighteen hours.

Eighteen hours of my husband's shoulders finally dropping. Eighteen hours of telling the kids we were getting out. Eighteen hours of feeling like the smartest person in the room. Of believing that months of obsessive planning had finally cracked the code.

Another email arrived.

Then I reread the fine print and every resource I could find that explained it.

The ICC coverage wasn't actually extra money. It was part of the same payout pot. If our contractor estimates hit the full policy limit, we'd get the payout, but lose ICC entirely. If we stayed under the maximum payout limit to preserve ICC, we'd be back to fighting about line items and receipts. The same nickel-and-dime hell we'd been trying to escape.

I stared at the screen, rereading the same paragraph until the words blurred.

"Wait!" I said out loud to no one. "Let me get this straight... You're telling me the house is basically totaled, but they're only paying repair costs? For repairs I'm not legally allowed to make!"

The whiplash wasn't just logistical. It was physical. Like celebrating that your crushed car would be covered, then learning they'd only pay for the dents to be popped out and painted. But the car's sides were crushed from all different angles and the engine wouldn't run anymore. Here I was, holding a substantial damage estimate letter that said the house most likely shouldn't be repaired and an insurance policy that would only pay for repairs.

Bile sat in my stomach begging to creep its way up my throat. I swallow it back down. The wave of control I'd just tasted was already dissolving like rice paper in my mouth. Fragile and thin. Replaced by the bitter taste of failure. I felt tricked, not by any person, but by a system that dangles solutions with invisible strings attached.

We had just told our kids. We had just told neighbors. We had just allowed ourselves to believe in something solid. I ached for the relief of the delusion.

Why couldn't we just have it a little bit longer?

My husband's face, when I explained the twist, didn't fall exactly. It tightened like a reflex. Like he was trying to hold space for both victory and defeat at once. I couldn't even cry. It was too sharp and sudden for tears. Just the throb of dizziness, the migraine of maybe-not-after-all.

"So what now?" he asked.
"I don't know," I said. "I honestly don't know."

How is this even possible? The same system that tells me I won't be able to legally repair, the one that would require demolition and elevation, turns around and says, but we're only paying for repair costs.

Repairs that I'm not allowed to do, if they cost what they actually cost, to be done professionally with permits.

They're telling me the house needs a complete rebuild, then handing me a check for what it would cost to swap out some baseboards. Part of the walls we had to tear out... *That they told me I should tear out.* And some cabinets. Not even the ones they missed while counting. Just the ones they felt like acknowledging later.

It's not even possible to rebuild a shell of our house 12 feet in the air with the insurance policy max without additional assistance.

Even if we qualify for mitigation grants to help bridge the gap in funds, no one is sure they are even going to exist anymore as programs are being shut down. We can't afford to risk being abandoned mid project even if we somehow scraped together the time, money and energy.

Even if we had actually wanted to stay.

I didn't want to game the system.
I didn't want more than we deserved.

I just wanted the system to acknowledge the obvious. That the home we owned, renovated, repaired, and tried so hard to save is gone. I wanted a number that meant we could walk away without borrowing from our future to repay the past.

But there is no totaling your flooded house and getting what it was worth. There is no clean break. No fair exchange. Just this, four vertical feet of house money and instruction to rebuild a life.

Well not even instructions, more like a demand. Honestly, I would welcome instructions. I want someone to tell me what I'm supposed to do. How I'm supposed to make this work for us.

We can't. That's the point. We've been trying to make things work for seven months.

Yet here I am, still explaining to people with clipboards why that should matter. Still arguing that we're not trying to scam anyone.

We're trying to survive this.

This isn't just a numbers game for us. This is our escape route and every time I think I've mapped the last detour, the road moves again.

We're still leaving this house. That hasn't changed. The substantial damage estimate is real. The ICC claim is still possible, even if it's not the payout I thought it was. But the way out just got longer again.

They need more evidence again.

And this time, I'm walking the exit route with whiplash. Trying to remember how to balance when the ground keeps shifting beneath my feet.

56.

Mother's Day

I woke softly and stepped into the kitchen for coffee, while everyone was still asleep, as I usually do. I sat down, listening for the distant sound of crinkling plastic. The telltale rustle of a body stirring on an air mattress. Whispering sheets. Stretching limbs. A household beginning to wake.

I let my mind wander in the best way.
Because today is Mother's Day.

I thought about how much time has passed. How years ago I was a young woman, just recently married, when we learned I was pregnant with Landon. The first of my friends to get married, the first to have a baby. We had just moved to Florida right before Landon was born. Full of hope and blank walls. Planting roots. Trying to build a home where our child would grow up.

I remember being scared when they let us bring him home. My husband and I sat in the parked car, looking at each other, still buckled in.

"So... they just let us bring him home?"
"We just... leave now?" I said.

We giggled, that nervous, stunned kind of laugh you make right before doing something you know you'll never fully be prepared for, but are already changed by.

The choice alone had changed us.
We knew we'd never be the same.

This tiny human, unable to hold his own head up, needed us to show him how to live in the world. And one day, if we did our job well enough, he might not need us in the same way. But we hoped that he would still turn to us. That we would build something so full of warmth, he'd know there would always be a soft place to land. Arms that could still hold him, *even if just for a moment.* Even if just long enough to remind him: You are known here.

Completely.

That would be success.

I thought about how badly we wanted to give him a sibling. And how hard it was when those two pregnancies didn't hold. A sibling can be your first lifelong friend. We wanted that for him. When we finally heard Fay's heartbeat, it felt like a victory. But we had to keep fighting. *I had to keep fighting.* My body had failed me before. This time, they said, it might fail differently.

But she made it.
We made it.

And our family was complete.

Our life grew more abundant as time moved forward. As height markings stacked on our door frame. The house was full of laughter. Our lives were full of little adventures. Hikes, swimming and bike rides. Craft projects galore. Humming and singing and dancing in the kitchen. Make-believe kingdoms mapped in sidewalk chalk and living room forts. Scraped knees healed with kisses.

***

I hear footsteps... spread out and slow.

Greg's stride.

He leans over the couch and kisses the top of my head. "Good morning. Happy Mother's Day!" he says, smiling.

He stumbles to the coffee maker, pours himself a mug, tops off mine. Then crouches in front of the mini fridge. The one sitting directly on the raw cement slab, and starts pulling out berries, eggs, and milk.

Fay emerges from the hallway.

"Good morning, good morning, I love you, good morning!" we both sing, almost in sync.

Fay nuzzles into me, squeezes tight. "Happy Mother's Day!" she beams, then skips to the whiteboard. She erases tomorrow and carefully replaces it with "Today." *Her best whiteboard-marker handwriting.* "Today is Mother's Day" surrounded by doodles.

The smell hits next. Weekend breakfast. Bacon crackling in one pan. French toast sizzling in another. Greg bouncing between two hot plates, orchestrating a stovetop symphony *of sorts.*

It smells like home.

Like the kind of Sunday mornings we used to have. Back when there was a backsplash, cabinets and counters.

Landon stumbles in, rubbing his eyes. "Happy Mother's Day." he mumbles sleepily, and leans in for a hug. Fay clears off the table. Pulls the tablecloth tight over the worn folding table. Landon washes the berries. Greg heaps food onto paper plates. I grab the plastic utensils.

We're not doing dishes today.
Dishes don't matter right now.

We sit and have family breakfast.
And for a moment, there's nothing missing.

57.

We'll Take the Exit However It Comes

We were continuing to settle into our new life in our damaged house.

I could hear the kids laughing more like they used to. They were enjoying more time together rather than feeling like they were stepping on each other's toes. They even started a movie marathon over the course of the last few weeks. They were watching superhero movies in chronological order.

Greg and I basked in the sounds of joy. We felt like we could start enjoying more moments too.

Things were still on-going, but there was a pattern to it that we had become accustomed to. Everything didn't feel as urgent as it used to once we accepted we had to wait.

Greg had received another achievement award at work. He was still delivering, still meeting his targets, still exceeding expectations.

I even planted green onions outside. Not that we had changed our mind about not wanting to plant roots here, *because we still didn't*. I planted them in a pot that could be moved instead of in the ground. Still living in the temporary. But it was nice to watch something grow again. To add herbs from our garden to the meals that we made.

I noticed a slight shift of chosen words from the kids lately. They used to say "when we move." Now they say "if we get to move."

"IF!"

Like they are trying to cling to hope they aren't sure is there anymore.

And I don't correct them like I used to. I don't reassure them that it's just a matter of when. That we just need to be patient because it will happen.

I think about "if" as well.
I just try not to say it out loud.

But it's always right after something, that finds a way of making us switch gears unexpectedly.

The day after I sent another email. The day after I put my foot down. The day after we think we have let go. That's when the ground shifts again. That's when the next thing shows up, not in triumph, but in a low, suspicious whisper.

This time, it was the day after we bought mattresses for the kids. Real ones, actual mattresses, not temporary ones filled with air. Not another sad layer of compromise we could deflate and shove in the closet. We bought them because we were tired of waiting. We didn't know how long we'd be stuck here, and the kids deserved to sleep without the slow hiss of sinking plastic under their backs.

It felt stupid and necessary.
A costly act of surrender.

We were staying. For now. So we tried to make it livable again.

And then, the next morning, the realtor texted. The one we had been talking to before Hurricane Helene. He might have a buyer. Just like that. Not a promise. Not a sure thing. But a sentence that said maybe, possibly, someone wanted the house that had broken us open.

And of course, of course, it would happen now. Now that we'd decided to stop waiting on hope. Now that we were settling in just enough to breathe. I didn't feel joy exactly. Instead, I felt braced. My body folded around the possibility like it was already protecting me from the fall.

But we've learned not to celebrate too early.

We've learned that paperwork gets lost.
That people change their minds.
That policies bend to fit convenience.

That even after the county says most likely "substantially damaged" the insurance company can shrug and say "not to us."

Then you are required to prove what has already been validated. *Not proved by you.* Not by the person who bought the materials, who installed them, and then had to tear it all out. *And who documented it all.*

How can they trust I'm holding a tape measure correctly in photos I sent to document linear feet? How can they be sure I am counting the cabinets in the photographs correctly, *even if the numbers are cross-referenced with the receipts.*

They want a professional... *not the licensed contractors that had already created estimates and quotes months ago either.*

New ones.
Prove it again.

That's what we were dealing with when the latest contractor came. He stood in the center of our gutted home and didn't flinch. He listened. He nodded. He said the quiet part out loud. The part no one else would confirm until now.

"Yeah, this is going to be a lot more than what they gave you."

He knew how insurance worked. Knew the numbers, the codes, the fights. He was helping other families too. Families who were exhausted. Who couldn't keep arguing with adjusters who wrote reports like they'd only half looked. He said he'd do what he could but it would take a couple weeks.

He explained how if we needed the repair work to be performed, that his company was still booking 9 months out. They have been consistently booked since the hurricanes. *It made sense.* Most of the contractors I had called this year had never even attempted to return my messages. Some had inboxes already at capacity. Out of the ones that did answer and schedule an appointment, only a fraction actually showed up when the day of the appointment came.

Hopefully it wouldn't come to that. He would assemble the estimate and help us submit and justify it to insurance. But even with his help, the whole process might take a few more months. We nodded. *We knew the drill.* We thanked him and then we continued to wait.

I still think this house shouldn't be standing.
I think we should be paid what we are owed and it should be torn down.

But *if* someone wants to buy the house before all of that?
If someone shows up with a number that lets us walk?
We'll take it.

Still, I won't let anyone walk into this blind.

If the buyer wants to fix the house, to salvage it, to pretend the studs still hold meaning, they need to understand what they're stepping into. Not just the gutted half house, but the loopholes. The technicalities. The minefield of agency and insurance definitions and permit codes.

Because yes, technically, the house can be repaired. Even after two floods. Even with the damaged innards stripped away. If they avoid having the permit trigger the County's official and final determination. If they do the work under the threshold. Piece by piece. They might make it through. They might build a version of home here that we couldn't.

One that we no longer want.

Who am I to say that's not allowed? That they aren't allowed to want something.

But I won't move forward without a warning. I won't hand off this house like it's just a fixer-upper. I won't let the next family walk in and think the hardest part is cosmetic.

I'll still make sure the buyer knows.
I won't let this be a secret.
Because It's a scar.

And I'm not passing it off without telling them exactly where it hurts.

58.

Flood Logic

I'm not sure people understand what I mean when I say "Flood Logic." How could they really? When I'm still learning its meaning myself.

What I do know is Flood Logic isn't just about disaster. It's about the adaptations you don't realize you've made until you're finally conscious enough to name them.

It's the way your body learns to breathe underwater not because it's meant to, but because it has to. You grow gills where lungs used to be tender. You get better at holding your breath through conversations. While wading through systems and swimming in shame. The flood becomes the logic. Everything outside of it feels unrecognizable.

I just did what I had to do...

What the flood waters required.
What the bureaucracy demanded.
What my family needed.

I developed flood logic without realizing I was developing anything at all. My nervous system made changes below conscious awareness because consciousness was too busy with immediate survival.

Here's what I'm learning, I can't fully see what I became because I'm still becoming it.

I still catch myself calculating exit routes no matter where I am, not out of pure paranoia, but out of practiced forethought. I am still documenting everything, photographing everything, and saving as much as I can. Not only out of compulsion, but because I've learned that evidence is oxygen.

I still hold multiple contingency plans in my head simultaneously. I still switch between them like navigating waves and currents. Plan A, Plan B, Plan Underwater, Plan For The Next Hurricane.

These aren't symptoms. These are skills.

When did I learn to read bureaucratic currents like weather patterns? When did I develop the ability to hold my family's safety with one arm, while bailing water with the other? When did scanning for threats become as automatic as checking for air?

I may have always done this to some extent.

My autistic brain learned early how to navigate a world not built for me. And, I've spent years learning how to continuously adapt after compiling traumas. The floods didn't change this. They didn't require me to learn a new skill. Instead, they required me to adapt faster, harder, in more directions at once. My existing skills got refined under pressure until adaptation became more automatic.

Trying not to drown wasn't new. But this version of myself, this version of flood logic, I learned it all in the underwater space. *Where different rules apply.*

Where holding your breath for months at a time is normal until you learn how to adapt. Where rebuilding a life out of salvaged parts is just Tuesday. Where fighting systems designed to exhaust you into submission becomes a specialized form of endurance swimming.

And I'm good at it now.

Really good.

I'm swimming toward what might be the surface, finally able to glimpse light filtering down through the water. I can imagine what it might feel like to walk again, instead of continuing to tread water. Sand and dirt clinging to my now webbed toes. What it might feel like to take a deep inhale of air while standing.

But I'm not there yet.

And honestly? *I'm not sure I'd trust it.* Because in flood logic, the surface can be a mirage. Just a trick of the current. And letting your guard down is how you drown. Trying to breathe in victory, just to risk having your lungs fill with water again. But I'm not holding my breath anymore. *I can't afford to.*

So I'm staying amphibious.

Gills ready.
Legs and feet ready.
Scanning the horizon for both shore and storm.

I don't owe anyone a graceful transition to something I haven't reached yet. I don't owe an explanation for keeping my gills when hurricane season just started. I don't owe anyone a performance of being "recovered" when I'm still actively managing the aftermath of the last flood. *And all the literal and figurative ones before.*

Flood logic isn't something you graduate from.
It's not even something you master.

It's learning to swim toward the surface through whatever is thrown your way, with skill instead of desperation. Trying to develop consciousness about your adaptations while still using them. Understanding that the ability to breathe underwater isn't a deficit.

But that it's an advantage in a world that floods.

Maybe that is the unexpected gift in all of this. What took me decades to develop through relentless survival will be passed down to my children.

They don't have to start from zero. Every pattern I broke meant they wouldn't have to. They won't inherit my drowning. They are beginning with my earned adaptations already in their foundation. Not my specific methods, but the permission and space to develop their own.

And that's the part I almost missed. I once thought their inheritance was my damage. But I overlooked that the ability to survive is also my legacy.

Our exit still looms, and hurricane season is here again. But I'm finally beginning to understand what I have evolved into. What it took to get me to this moment. And what will carry me through the moments to come.

Of course, I wish my life didn't require any of this. But I'm no longer sorry for being the way I am.

The logic remains.
Adaptive.
Essential.

Mine.

EPILOGUE

For the ones not sure what comes next.

If you made it all the way here,
I want you to know I don't take that lightly.

I don't know your exact story.
Maybe something in these pages met you where you are.
Or reminded you of where you have been.

I won't pretend to know what you are carrying,
but I'd like to thank you for staying with me.

I assume you came here hoping for a clean ending.
A moment of triumph.
Where the struggles fade into dust,
and all that's left is the light of victory.

Even after the warning,
something inside you still wished,
the story wrapped itself in a bow.

But I have no complete victory to offer.
I didn't write this in the safety of "after."

I wrote this while still sleeping on an air mattress.

While still fighting systems.
While still uncertain about our future.

I wish I could promise you a happily-ever-after.

But what I can give you is this.
My ongoing choice to keep moving forward.
Even without knowing where it leads.

Because struggles don't disappear,
just because we overcome one battle.
Or even two.

Success doesn't always live in the end.

It lives in how we stand *or swim*.
In how we decide to live.
In how we keep breathing.

Even when the fight is far from over.
Even when the odds are stacked against us.

I can't give you resolution,
but I can ask you to keep going too.

Keep showing up.
Keep moving.
Even if the road is long
and the finish line isn't in sight.

I can remind you that your voice matters.
That your actions and choices matter.

Even if you don't want to be where you are.
Especially if you don't.

Maybe that's success.
Simply refusing to be finished.

Flood Logic is a part of me.
I think it will always be.
My struggles shape me,
but they aren't the only things that define me.

Yes I am still in the thick of it all.
Yes I am a survivor.

But I am so many other things as well.
And so are you.

We are the compilation of our experiences,
our choices,
characteristics and beliefs.

The world is constantly changing.
And so are we.

So this is where I am now.
Where I think most of us are.
Still breathing.
Still becoming.

AUTHOR'S NOTE

If you devoured the pages of this book, I'd like to share something about the way these words reached you.

I often write the way I speak. Pausing to carefully choose my words. Providing detailed context. And building complete pictures.

Throughout my life, I've watched people dismiss these same thoughts when I speak them aloud. Distracted by the way I hold my body, where my eyes wander and the rhythm of my speech. They hear anxiety when I'm offering analysis. Drama where I'm trying to be precise.

But in writing, my words are finally taken at face value.

As an autistic person, I've spent decades watching my spoken words get filtered through assumptions about how communication "should" sound. Yet here, in these pages, you met my thoughts directly. You followed my patterns. You found meaning in my methods.

If you connected with this book, I invite you to pause next time someone's communication doesn't match your expected norm. When we close ourselves off to different ways of thinking and sharing, we limit our worldview.

I urge you to consider being the kind of person who offers buttered noodles. Who provides simple care without demanding that someone reshape themselves to receive it. *Different doesn't necessarily mean less than or wrong.*

The impact of truly being seen and heard might be what someone has spent their whole life craving.

-Ashley

www.ingramcontent.com/pod-product-compliance
Lightning Source LLC
Chambersburg PA
CBHW011219120626
46545CB00010B/3072